To Carol &
with gratitude,
friendship & fellowship in the
Lord over the years —

DESERT HARVEST

God Bless you always

Arthur W. Dodd

2 COR 12^9

DESERT HARVEST

BY

Canon Arthur Dodds

Collectors' Books Limited

Published by Collectors' Books Limited,
Bradley Lodge,
Kemble
Cirencester. GL7 6AD
Tel. 0285 770 239   Fax: 0285 770 896

© Canon Arthur Dodds, 1993
ISBN 0-946604-05-3

Illustrations:

PREFACE

by the Rt. Rev. John Perry
Bishop of Southampton

J.B.Phillips, in the preface to his translation of the Acts of the Apostles, *The Young Church in Action* says: "These men did not make acts of faith, *they believed;* they did not say their prayers, they *really prayed.* They did not hold conferences on psychosomatic medicine, they *simply healed the sick.*" As I read *Desert Harvest,* these words came to mind. There is an authentic ring about this book and I found it compulsive reading.

Arthur Dodds has the enviable capacity to write as he talks, and this he does with no little skill and vivacity. The story of his life is told with refreshing honesty and self-deprecating humour. He charts a fascinating and often gripping account of his wartime escapades, to be followed by his time at university and theological college. Then came ordination and contrasting periods of parish ministry, culminating in the founding of Harnhill. Always generous and perceptive in his reflections on events and encounters with the very many people he has met over the years, the author's enthusiasm and zest for life are constantly in evidence.

The word pictures that Arthur Dodds paints reveal a man of faith, who walks humbly with his God. A walk that he and Letty, his wife, have shared together throughout their fulfilling time together. Here is the story of a man who has known the hand of God upon him from earliest years. His adventurous spirit, coupled with his recognition of human frailty as well as potential, have combined to instil within him a longing to be ever more available to his Lord and to the leading of the Holy Spirit. He stands firmly in the line of men and women down the centuries who have dared to trust God, often against human odds, and to live by faith.

Now in his 70s he could justifiably put on his carpet slippers and begin to live at an easier pace. But not so! On he goes with the fast-growing ministry at Harnhill very much at heart. The story of the birth and early years of Harnhill is told with pride and immense thankfulness for the many who have caught and shared the vision for a Centre for Christian Healing and a resource for teaching and training for the wider Church. In its short history many people have passed through its welcoming doors and experienced, through the care and counsel of this community, the unconditional healing love of Jesus Christ.

Desert Harvest will be a challenge and a tonic to all who read it. For here is a man who places prayer as his constant priority and always points away from himself to the power and sufficiency of the living God.

✝John Perry
Bishop of Southampton
January, 1993

CHAPTER 1

THE BURNING BUSH

Just after midnight on 31st May 1942, a Wellington Bomber was shot down over the Western Desert by a Messerschmitt 109 fighter. Nearly fifty years later, now heavily involved in a Centre for Christian Healing, I have been moved and encouraged to write this book. Deserts are barren places, but with a little water, as with God's grace, they can beget new life from unseen seeds. This has been my experience with wildernesses.

I was the navigator and bomb aimer, then called the observer, of the Wellington bomber that night. As a crew, we had already completed some twenty sorties under our experienced skipper and first pilot, Bill Astell DFC, later killed on the famous Dam Buster raid. We anticipated an easy trip. Our target was a new German airfield near Derna, opened in preparation of Rommel's big push, which was expected at any moment. We were light-hearted and cheerful as we set out, anticipating little 'flak' on this run, unlike the heavy concentrations we usually encountered over Benghazi Harbour, the main supply port for the Axis troops in the Western Desert, or over the German submarine base at Salamis, near Piræus in Greece across the Mediterranean. We had returned from there one night with thirty-six holes in the aircraft, according to the ground crew who had to mend them.

We had just completed our first bombing run on the airfield and were going round to drop our second stick of bombs when the rear gunner shouted a warning over the intercom, of an enemy fighter approaching. As he finished speaking, tracer bullets ripped through the aircraft. The second pilot received a rain of bullets across his chest and slumped to the floor. The rear gunner reported his turret was out of action and on fire, and also that he was slightly wounded. Another hail of bullets ripped through the plane just above me as I lay on the floor in the nose, in the bomb aimer's position.

I understood the literal meaning of the expression 'petrified with fear', I found I just could not move. Then came into my mind the last line of a hymn, which we had often sung in school: "Trust in God and do the right". I repeated it over and over again to myself. As I repeated the first part: "Trust in God" my fear eased as my mind turned to God and away from fear. I felt calm. "Do the right;" I must help the second pilot.

The skipper was on the intercom. He had jettisoned the rest of the bombs as our hydraulic system had been hit and he could not maintain height. He told us to get on our parachutes, in preparation for baling out. The second pilot was now on his feet and said he was all right. Two years later I was to learn that his elbow was shot to pieces and his heart had been saved by a torch in his breast pocket. As I went back to get my 'chute, panic returned. I repeated the line of the hymn and became calm once more: I went forward to help the second pilot get his 'chute on. While I was there I told the skipper I would try to put out the fire which I had noticed in the starboard wing near the nacelle petrol tank, if he would try to maintain height. I kept on repeating the line of the hymn to myself as I played the tiny jet of the fire extinguisher onto the source of the raging flames. After a while the fire began to die down and was nearly out when I felt the aircraft's wheels, which were dangling loose, touch the ground.

I just had time to brace myself before the crash. I was thrown forward into the pilot's cabin and Bill yelled: "Get out, quick!" I hurried back and threw my secret papers on the fire which had flared up again. I collected a map, a small escape compass, my loaded revolver and my water bottle, which had leaked and now contained only about a third of a pint. As I scrambled out of the burning aircraft, the skipper shouted: "Run for it!"

"What about the others?" I called.

"They all baled out" he said, as he began to run. I poked my head into the rear door of the plane and yelled and looked, just to make sure. I then ran about eighty yards and threw myself down behind a boulder beside Bill, just as the aircraft exploded. That was the end of our adventures in "R for Roger" and the beginning of a new one, which was to be of great significance to me.

All my life I had had a niggling thought deep inside me that I ought to become a clergyman, but I had funked the idea. As we started on this long walk, knowing that it was likely to be a very long one (I estimated about one hundred and twenty miles), I thought that here was an ideal opportunity to think and pray this thing through and come to a decision, one way or the other. Bill and I did not talk a great deal to each other except when necessary to take decisions. In any case, neither of us were chatterers.

The terrain was difficult in parts, with broken, craggy rocks. The concept of the desert consisting only of smooth sand was soon dispelled. We could see quite well in the bright moonlight, although shapes could be deceptive as we discovered when we crept up to what we thought was a Bedouin encampment, only to find that it was a rock formation.

As we walked I thought of Jesus when He was in the desert for forty days and nights. I sensed him very close, as though He was walking with me. I talked to Him in my imagination about this business of being a parson and asked Him to make it clear to me.

Bill and I walked and walked, urging each other on as first one and then the other would stagger, especially in the later stages. For six nights we walked, with no food and little water. As the first night gave way to dawn, we found a lovely cave, high in the side of a wadi. I felt sure it had been used by a hermit centuries before, as I found one ear of unripe corn growing near the mouth of the cave. We shared it between us. I also found a packet of wine gums in the pocket of my battledress jacket, which gave us four each. That was my last food for five days, but already it was water for which we craved, rather than food. That cave gave us ideal shelter from the heat of the sun and the prying eyes of German planes or patrols that first day.

We were not so fortunate on the third day. We had decided to take the risk of heading towards the coast road, where the German line of communications would be, in the hope of finding water and food, or even hijacking a vehicle. As it began to get light at the end of the first night of walking, all we could see was unbroken desert, miles and miles of it. Eventually with the light which was now quite bright, we had to opt for the only possible cover there was, an isolated desert thorn bush, with no leaves but plenty of prickles. We pushed ourselves under it and fell into an exhausted sleep.

At noon I awoke conscious that the bush was giving little shelter from the sun which was now overhead. All around for mile upon mile was nothing but desert. Above there was nothing but the vast expanse of blue sky. I suddenly felt totally exposed to God, completely naked before my Maker. He looked down into my innermost being and said: "Stop running away. You know very well I have been calling you to be a parson."

"But", I protested, "I have not done well in my studies and I am so terribly shy, I could never stand up and preach to a lot of people. I'm just not good enough in any way." He cut in and declared: "I will give you strength for anything I have for you to do." I tried to think of an argument against that and couldn't find one. After a while, I said: "All right, I promise you that if, and when I get back, I will send in my name as an ordination candidate, but it will have to be up to You; I can't do it alone." Almost immediately, I heard a car coming to a stop and a door shut. A German officer was standing about one hundred and fifty yards away surveying the landscape with binoculars. Bill was still asleep. I got out my revolver thinking: "It is my duty to shoot him." But, with my shaky hand and at that distance, I knew there was little, if any, chance of killing him. It would only give us away. I kept my revolver pointing towards him and watched him as he surveyed the countryside. Then he got into the car and his driver drove away. At any rate we must be near the supply route and our bush did give us visual protection, which was confirmed by the number of German aircraft that flew over that day.

We did not leave that bush until it was almost dark. It must have been around midnight when we came across several German trucks, with troops sleeping on the ground around them We quietly explored the trucks and ground, hoping to find food or water. One truck had an outside pocket or container. The lid squeaked as we opened it and a soldier two yards away stirred, but slept on. There was a tin inside which came out without noise. There was also a wrapped loaf of bread. The rustle of the paper as we tried to get it out, caused two or three soldiers to stir. We waited until they were quiet again, to have another try. Unfortunately, the opening of the pocket was slightly smaller than the width of the loaf and there was no way we could get it out without waking the soldiers. We had to leave it. Freedom was more important than bread.

As soon as we got a safe enough distance away, we examined the tin. Peppers! Bill opened it with my penknife. The unfamiliar taste made me retch, so Bill ate them all. My great craving was for liquid. I was not really hungry, but I imagined myself plunging into a swimming pool of fresh orange juice and drinking and drinking. Occasionally I thought of Jesus crying:

"I thirst" from the cross.

As the fourth day began to dawn, the light came quickly as we were anxiously looking for a shelter. Suddenly we came upon a German camp in a slight hollow. A nearby tent had a good-sized shrub next to it. We made for the shrub as reveille sounded. As we did so, we noticed a jerrican near the tent door. Although there were slight stirrings within the tent, Bill picked up the can, opened it and found water. He took a couple of good swigs and handed it on to me to do the same. We put the can back, got ourselves into the shrub and looked forward to the rest of the water that night We slept reasonably well in spite of the noises and comings and goings. One soldier stopped right by the shrub and we thought he must have spotted us. Then we felt a splash; he urinated on the bush right over our heads and walked on.

We waited that night for the two senior N.C.O.s, as we assumed them to be, to get to sleep in the tent. They had obviously fed well for they belched loudly and often, passed wind and talked until nearly midnight. When at last all was quiet, we came out, took the jerrican, now unfortunately barely a quarter full, and headed south. We soon found ourselves walking down a track through the middle of the camp and then between lines of various vehicles: trucks, tanks and cars. It was presumably a maintenance depot. One tank had only just come in, with the dust still settling, the men getting out and talking. They must have seen us in the moonlight, but probably assumed we were German soldiers taking a jerrican of petrol to a truck. Once well clear of the camp, we took a good swig of the water and pressed on. Two swigs later the water was gone and we got rid of the can. The next day we hid in a shallow wadi. We were obviously near the front line as the wadi was shelled by our guns morning and evening. By now we were living skeletons. I looked at Bill as he lay there. His skin was like thin yellow parchment, stretched tight across his skull-like face, unnaturally hooking down his nose. I knew that I must look the same.

We waited until it was quite dark that sixth night before we headed East, hoping to reach our own troops before dawn. After a while there was a fair amount of German activity: we found ourselves amongst small groups of troops, talking quietly as they worked on something, perhaps laying mines. As we made our way between two of these groups, we were challenged and Bill, who spoke good German, said: "We are the signallers" and kept going. We came to clearer ground. I stumbled on a rock and fell as a tracked vehicle came from the east, firing tracer. Bill said: "Give me your revolver, it must be an allied patrol coming through". He went off, firing my revolver and calling out to try and attract attention. I though he was more likely to attract a bullet. After the shooting had died down, I walked around calling out, "Bill, Bill!!" in a sort of loud hoarse whisper. Apparently, I learned later, he had been doing the same, calling me before giving up and heading on east. He walked through a South African minefield, and was delighted to be greeted by, "Hey! You can't walk there it's mined!"

I also headed east and, as I went along a track, was suddenly challenged by a German sentry and commanded to halt and identify myself. I stopped absolutely still and said nothing. A shot rang out. A bullet ricocheted off a nearby rock and hit me on the upper lip, knocking me down, I lay there. The German came down the track a few yards, made a remark to another soldier and returned to his post. I decided I must stay absolutely still for some time. As I lay there, I wondered to what church I should offer myself as a candidate for ordination when I got back. My father was an anglican vicar so I knew something of the snags and failures of the Church of England. While in the R.A.F., I had taken the opportunity to try other denominations without being unduly impressed. I decided on the Church of England. If there were things wrong, it was up to me to do what I could to put them right.

All had been quiet for twenty minutes. It was time to move. I retraced my steps as quickly and quietly as I could and then headed north towards El Sollûm, which had been in Allied hands the last time I had heard the news in the mess. I was walking now in a kind of faint, unable to hear or see other than in a fog, unless I stopped and consciously swallowed, not that there was anything to swallow. I did this as I was walking along a track and suddenly heard an excited jabbering of Italians; these soldiers saw me quite clearly in the moonlight. I could see now that there was a sort of shallow quarry on either side of the track and the Italians were rummaging around as though scavenging, as if the position had recently been occupied. I quickly jumped down to the right and headed east, making my way from bush to bush, playing hide-and-seek with the Italian soldiers. As I was climbing out of the quarry and looking back to see if any of them were following me, I walked right into a sentry and collapsed at his feet. Beyond him, I later discovered, was no-man's-land, with our lines only two hundred yards away.

I was a prisoner. I had failed again, as so often in the past. But this time it had been worth it. I was now certain of God's call. Moses had had a burning bush experience in the desert. Without comparing myself with Moses, so had I. Whenever my faith might waver in the future, my mind would go back to that thorn bush and God's promise: "I will give you strength for anything I have for you to do". He has kept his promise. I have noticed it most when I have felt completely inadequate and weak. As God said to St Paul: "my power is greatest when you are weak". (2 Cor. 12.9 G.N.B.)

CHAPTER 2

A SICKLY CHILD

My ability to survive such a desert walk would have seemed unlikely a few years earlier as I was a sickly child. At least I did not give my attractive Yorkshire mother any problems at birth. When she came down early to light the fire in the huge rectory at Risely, Bedfordshire on 25th November 1920, I decided it was time to arrive and did so in a hurry. The midwife hardly had time to get there. I would probably have been called hyperactive today, but then they just gave me the nickname of "Twiddly" because I was always on the move and unable to stay still. My elder brother, Carter, and later my two younger brothers, Michael and John, were much nicer children.

My first worrying habit was my tendency to go into black fits of tearless rage. A large motherly cook was the only one who could cope with them: she would pick me up by the feet in one large hand and smack my bottom hard with the other, causing me to yell out and then cry with tears, and so break the fit. Later she would compensate me for this harsh treatment by giving me a matchbox full of currants. I liked her and spent hours crawling round the large kitchen floor.

When I was vaccinated for smallpox, I became very ill and my life hung in the balance for a few weeks. It was assumed that the scalpel had been dirty, but now I wonder whether I was born with the same allergic conditions with which my two grandsons are afflicted. They were not allowed to be vaccinated because of their allergy. I still have a scarred and pitted left arm.

My next crisis was when I toddled into my parents' bedroom and found a bottle of sleeping pills on my mother's dressing table. I discovered they had a sweet sugar coating, so I sucked them until they got bitter and then swallowed quickly. They found me in a deep coma lying in front of the dressing table, the bottle half empty, and nursed me back to life with a daily ration of 3 teaspoons of brandy and white of egg; perhaps that was another of Cook's remedies.

I went to the village school for just a few months. My only memory is of being taken one day with my elder brother on a toboggan through the snow, drawn by my father. Even during those two or three months, I was often away through ill health and then I was stopped from going to school altogether. It was diagnosed that I had "glands". I never did discover what it meant except that I was not allowed to go to school for several years, but wandered on my own through the fields, climbing trees and finding things: birds' nests, conkers, blackberries and mushrooms. I gained a great love of the countryside. It also gave me a terrible sense of guilt because I was not at school and this was probably a contributory factor to my acute shyness, which remained with me well into adulthood. I avoided the other boys and girls who did go to school and had a great sense of inferiority. When sent on errands to the butcher, I would go a long way round through the fields to avoid passing the school.

Once I broke my left arm at the elbow by vaulting with a pole over the tennis net and just catching my heel on the top of the net. Years later I was to high jump and pole vault for Oxford University, without breaking my arm but breaking the pole on one occasion. The doctor had a theory that, to mend the fracture, I should carry a small suitcase full of bricks around with me for several weeks. This would be better than putting my arm in plaster. As a result of this treatment I have never been able to straighten my left elbow completely. According to my elder brother, who later played cricket for Essex, this accounted for my bat not being perfectly straight during the frequent family games on the lawn. Whenever he could, my father would join in and coach us. He had played good cricket at Oxford and at Torquay; he was an attacking front-foot batsman and also a bowler equally effective with either arm.

Asthma has, for me, been a life-long affliction. Not until I was thirty-two and went to a specialist in London, did I discover that I was allergic to everything imaginable: fabric dusts, pollens, moulds, animals and many foods. This latter may have accounted for my constant indigestion. Also I was frequently plagued with colds, bronchitis and catarrh which gave me bad earache and left me partially deaf in one ear.

My first encounter with the living God came about through my asthma. We were living at Wymington, near Rushden in Bedfordshire in a damp vicarage. To help me catch up with my schooling my parents had sent me to Bedford Modern School when I was nine or ten years old. Each day when I was reasonably well, I would cycle the five miles to Sharnbrook station on a terrible second-hand bike to catch the train to Bedford. One snowy morning I had hardly gone a mile when I skidded and fell off while pedalling up a hill. The driver of a car overtaking me just managed to stop in time and he encouraged me to return home because of the road conditions. When I got home my asthma was bad; usually it had cleared by the time I reached Sharnbrook as a result of the exercise. I was put to bed by my mother, feeling guilty and wondering if I was malingering. But my asthma was genuine enough: I was fighting for every breath. I caught sight of the terror in my mother's eyes. She was quite obviously afraid that each breath was going to be my last; I wondered the same! "She thinks I am going to die", I thought. Then, suddenly, a wonderful assurance flooded into my mind: "Even if I die, I shall still be within the care of my Heavenly Father". I must have owed this knowledge to my parents, but it was good to experience it at first-hand for myself. Relaxing in this new-found trust in God's care, my breathing eased a little and I was soon asleep. This was a lesson which was to prove valuable later when involved in the Ministry of Christian Healing: namely the encouragement of people to focus their minds and hearts on the greatness and the love of God, rather than on the sickness or the problem.

Through my boyhood years and beyond, I was prone to faint. At the morning services at Wymington my brothers used to bet cigarette cards on which hymn we would get to before I went over. Some of my faints were quite dramatic, as when queuing for a matinee at the Stratford-on-Avon Theatre in my teens; I went down with such a bang on the pavement that the whole queue was alarmed. I was soon on my feet again and wondered what all the fuss was about. I enjoyed the play!

In 1932 we moved to the lovely vicarage of Hatton near Warwick. After one term at Warwick School, where my brother's prowess at cricket soon took him into the first XI, I was sent away to a small prep school - Coombe Florey in Somerset - in the hope that my health would improve. It did help, although I recall often being in bed from where I could hear the other boys playing outside in the sun. During one such time I can remember thinking: "Although I am missing the fun, yet these times have made me pray and think about Jesus". The words from Romans 8.28 spoke to me from an early age: "We know that in everything God works for good in those who love him". I felt closer to Jesus as a friend during that period of my life than at any other; I was twelve. The young Welsh matron was kind to me and encouraged me in my faith. She also lent me the Complete Works of Shakespeare which I waded through in time: the first book I ever read.

After a year at Coombe Florey, I went to Taunton School on a clergy bursary. I began to get some consecutive teaching and enjoyed the games. But I still went across to the school hospital twice a week for constipation, still wetted my bed, still had asthma and bad catarrh, which gave me acute sinusitis. I was late returning to school one term because I had developed a murmur on the heart. I felt reasonably well when sitting or lying down but when I stood up, I immediately fell to the ground in a faint.

In the middle of taking School Certificate in November 1938, having only got four credits in the Summer and needing five for matriculation, I was struck down by nephritis. I had not been feeling well, but that was nothing unusual. Then one morning my face was so puffed up that my eyes were almost closed and I was sent across to the school hospital. The doctor told me I had nephritis which meant staying in bed for some time; when he had gone I wept, I had failed my matric again. I asked the nurse and she told me that nephritis was a kidney complaint, normally only contracted by middle-aged drunks.

I missed the whole of the next term, spending much of it in St Luke's Hospital for clergy families, in London. They cleared up the illness and I then enjoyed just over a year of reasonable health. I passed my School Certificate, played cricket, rugby and tennis for the school and did well in athletics.

In 1940 I volunteered for air crew in the R.A.F. I did not mention my various illnesses but was nearly caught out by my hearing when the doctor tested my bad ear by holding a pocket watch well away from me and bringing it slowly nearer. After a while I realised I ought to be able to hear it ticking that close to my ear, so I said "Now!" as I had been instructed. When he tested my good ear I could hear the ticking at twice the distance. So, when he tested my bad ear again, I said "Now!" at what I judged to be the same distance as for the good ear. He was satisfied and passed me as "A 1."

CHAPTER 3

IN THE BAG

The early days of captivity were grim. When I collapsed at the feet of that last sentry, I was soon surrounded by soldiers. A German officer came and briefly interrogated me. I gave him my name, rank and number. I was relieved of my R.A.F. watch and searched for anything else without success. I was taken a little way and put in a cave, which sloped downwards, with a guard on the entrance. In the morning I was given a drink of water; it was all too little but then, they were short as well. I was also given some bread but could manage to eat very little of it, my mouth just could not cope with such dry food. That night I was forced to walk under guard and I kept stumbling and falling until a Tommy who had been captured and was being taken back with me, put his arm round me and helped me along. Eventually we reached a van in which there were two German soldiers; we were given some freshly cooked risotto. It was delicious; so moist and warm, it slipped down easily. I must have looked ill as they let me have a second helping.

At first light we were driven off in the van, arriving a few hours later at a wire pen in the middle of the desert, where other allied troops were incarcerated. The sun was hot, and water very short. The next day some of us were transported to Derna Castle where the courtyards were packed with prisoners of war, many in a poor way. I was further interrogated, this time by a pompous Italian major. I gave him my name, rank and number:

"What were you doing behind the lines?" No reply.

"You are a spy!" I denied this. He became extremely annoyed and abusive. There seemed to be no harm in telling him that I had been shot down and had walked a long way to get back to our troops. He still was not satisfied and wanted to know more. I remained silent while he ranted and raged, drawing his revolver and threatening to shoot me. He didn't, but struck me and had me thrown back into the castle courtyard where the conditions were filthy.

I slumped against a wall on the hard floor on which we slept. Not far away was a Gurkha soldier with his right arm severed at the wrist and a rough blood-stained bandage over the stump. He sat there looking down at where his hand had been, and tears silently trickled down his cheek. Within me I cried for him too, wishing there was something I could do for him. After a while I wanted to spend a penny and asked where the toilet was. I was told and it turned out to be a small room from which the double door was missing. Inside, nearly the whole floor space was covered by a huge pile of excreta. I spent my penny on the edge. As I was leaving, two soldiers carried in a third who had had his legs blown off. They held him over the pile while he added his contribution to it.

Two days later, many of the officers were bundled into cattle trucks for the long, bumpy and dusty drive to a PoW camp outside the town of Benghazi, and the comparative comfort of wooden bunk beds. I was still very ill. An army officer nearby befriended me and gave the one item he had managed to grab from his tent when he had been captured: a spare shirt. Mine was badly torn. He also found an army doctor among the prisoners. In addition to dysentery I was beginning to swell alarmingly from the legs upward; my skin was as tight as a drum. I felt that if I pricked it with a pin, I would burst like a balloon. It was a very frightening sensation: the doctor diagnosed beri-beri. He said that I ought to eat little and often, but there was nothing he could do about that: "you will probably survive" he concluded.

After a few days, I was removed on the pretext that as an R.A.F. officer I was to be given better accommodation. I was taken in a small truck to a cultivated area of fruit trees and vegetables, among which was a group of wooden huts. I was escorted into one of these and put in a small room with two beds and chairs. I was told to make myself comfortable and asked if I would like a cup of coffee. I eagerly replied in the affirmative, thinking that my luck was changing. I went over to the barred window in front of which a guard walked up and down, but beyond was the refreshing sight of green trees and cultivation. The coffee arrived and it was hot and sweet, I drank it with relish. Feeling dozy, I lay down on the luxury of a real bed and was soon asleep.

When I awoke, I found that an army officer lay on the other bed. He introduced himself in excellent English, but with a foreign accent, as an officer in the Free French Tank Regiment. He told me how he had been caught and asked me how I had been captured. I told him a little and then, finding myself unusually talkative, went on to tell him a great deal about my home and family. He kept bringing the conversation back to where I was shot down, what the target was, where was the airfield I had flown from. I kept compulsively talking about my home and family. After an hour or more, lunch was brought in and then some more coffee. Again I felt dozy and had another sleep; when I awoke I found myself alone once more. The next day I was taken back to the Benghazi camp, and a day or two later was flown with others to Italy.

Some weeks later, in a permanent camp, I related these experiences to a British intelligence officer who was vetting everyone to ensure that we had no stool-pigeon in our midst. He told me that I had been given the truth drug in the coffee to make me talk to that supposed Free French officer.

On arrival in Italy, we spent about ten days in a transit camp at Bari. Initially, our batch of about forty officers was herded together outside a wooden hut by some friendly and harmless Italian guards. Their main attribute, in my recollection, was their ability to break out into wonderful operatic arias. In the evening, as the light was beginning to fade, the camp commandant, a fascist major, came strutting towards us in breeches and leggings and carrying a long horsewhip. He ordered us into the hut. We refused. The senior officer among us, acting as spokesman, pointed out that the hut was already full and the windows blocked up; we would be likely to suffocate. We gave him our assurance that we would behave if he would allow us to sleep outside. No, every person had to be in a hut before dark. He strutted and shrieked and cracked his whip. He ordered about a dozen guards to fix bayonets and force us in. They prodded us, pleading with us to go in, then the camp commandant got behind the guards and began whipping them to make them use their bayonets properly. Our senior officer suggested we should go in for the sake of the guards and so we squashed inside. The only toilet was a large bowl in the middle of the floor, already full. I don't remember that night; I think I passed out.

The next day a number of other prisoners went by train to permanent camps and we moved into a reasonable hut with wooden bunk beds. That night a prisoner was shot as he walked towards the wire asking where the toilet was. On Sunday an R.C. army chaplain organised a simple ecumenical service of readings, prayers and talk. He asked me to read a lesson. About twenty or thirty of us stood round in the open air; it was a great blessing. A few days later we were sent to Chieti, my residence for the next fifteen months.

Life "in the bag" began to improve once we had reached this permanent camp at Chieti: "Campo Concentramento P.G. 75". A tarmac roadway went straight through the middle of the camp from the guardhouse entrance to the cookhouse and assembly hall at the other end. Standing back from this main roadway, on each side, there were two large single storey concrete buildings. In addition, a smaller building near the entrance acted as the sick quarters. In each of the four main buildings there were three hundred prisoners. There were no doors but a passage right through the building with a series of open rooms or spaces on either side. At the end were hole-in-the-ground toilets and wash basins, but little water. Right round the perimeter of the camp was a high wall on top of which were a number of sentry boxes with machine guns.

As it was a brand new camp, we did not have the bed-bug and lice problems of other camps. Each of us was thoroughly fumigated and de-loused on arrival. None of us had expected to be taken prisoner although we had thought of the possibility of being wounded or killed. Some of the aircrew on our squadron had written letters to be sent to relatives in the event of their being killed. I had written one to my parents just before the squadron left for a short spell in Malta at the height of the siege. Our task was to fit in as many bombing raids as possible on the German airfields in Sicily before our own aircraft were destroyed on the ground. It was a humbling experience to witness the courageous and resilient spirit of the Maltese people, whose homes and towns were just piles of rubble and who were deprived of food, water, electricity, soap and the other normal everyday commodities. Yet, they lined the route and cheered us all the way as our old bus bumped its way over the pitted road to Luqua airfield each evening for our night raids. Now a month later, here I was in the bag, although the possibility of becoming a prisoner of war had never occurred to me. We had to adjust and seek to make the best of it.

Before long, life in camp became highly organised. Lectures were laid on and soon you could study almost any subject you chose under a qualified person. Padre Chutter, an anglican, discovered eleven of us were interested in the possibility of ordination. He sent our names to the Advisory Council in England and organised a course of lectures suitable for our ordination exams. He devised a structure for our devotional life, of morning and evening prayer, a mid-week Communion and Compline twice a week. On Sunday we joined the camp services; these were so popular that within a few months virtually all the prisoners attended the morning service. Some of those on the ordination course later went on to Germany and were able to take the first part of the General Ordination Exam there, and pass.

Food was a central subject for all and most of us spoke from time to time of the meal we were going to have when we got home. Meanwhile, our diet consisted of one small roll of very indifferent flour and a cup (or rather, a home made tin mug) of ersatz coffee for breakfast, a bowl of swill or vegetable soup for lunch with some fruit if available, and a thicker soup in the evening, which included our daily ration of pasta or rice, again with fruit if available. Twice a week we would have in addition a small piece of cheese and once a week a little bit of meat would be in the evening swill. The main vegetable in the soup for much of the year was pumpkin. For the first two months there was no salt; there can be few less palatable dishes than pumpkin soup without salt. Much later we occasionally got a Red Cross parcel, or rather, one between two. That was bliss. Some had a good tuck in; others eked it out for as long as possible.

I was still unwell. I developed jaundice and, following that, continued to have acute stomach pains. After a while I saw a young Italian doctor: he thought I probably had a stomach ulcer and prescribed two plates of plain boiled rice a day instead of the other food. After about two months with no improvement I put myself back on the ordinary food.

One night as I lay tossing on my bunk, my stomach pain was particularly severe: I longed to finish it. I wanted to reach for my knife at the head of my bed, plunge it into the pain and commit suicide. As I thought about it, I suddenly had a clear picture of Jesus hanging on the Cross, and thought of the much worse pain that He had endured. "So what?" I reasoned, "the fact that He had endured awful pain then, doesn't help me now," and yet it did. Somehow it helped me to endure mine and get to sleep.

It was not very long before we had our first stage show in the Assembly Hall. Two army officers in bunks near mine were keen on acting and wrote a melodrama called "Ditchwater's Dilemma or Barchester Towers". As I was young and fair skinned, I was persuaded to be the heroine in a long white dress made from sheeting with a blonde wig made from string. My punchline, addressed to the villain, was:

"No! No! You can't do that to me!" With plenty of cheers, laughter, booing and hissing, the show went down well. I am glad to say that in spite of my female part, no improper advances were made to me off-stage. In fact I only heard of one possible case of homosexuality the whole time we were in camp.

Much later the Italians let us have some musical instruments, and concerts were performed. The conductor was Tony Baines. Nearly a quarter of century later, I invited the Cheltenham Sunday Players to perform an orchestral concert in Chedworth Church in the Cotswolds. Imagine my surprise when, on the night, I found that the conductor was none other than Tony Baines.

There was a good deal of humour in the camp and much poking of fun at our captors. On the whole we were optimistic, although rumours of the advances and defeats of allied troops could quickly cause spirits to rise or fall.

It was cold that winter of 1942-43, but we survived with our one short blanket, which may have been long enough for the short Italians, but not for the average Briton. When we had been marched to the camp on arrival, I had picked up a well-made sack lying at the side of the road, out of it I had made myself a pair of trousers to replace my tattered khaki drills. My tailoring achievements were, however, nothing when compared to the skill of some of the others. One R.A.F. officer made a wireless set out of bits of tin and smuggled parts. Clocks were numerous, none of this with the help of the fascist captain, nominally the second in command of the camp, but, in effect, he ran it under the figurehead of the major. The captain was a sadist and enjoyed making life unpleasant for us if he could. He withheld information from the Red Cross, hence our lack of parcels, until we had a visit from a Red Cross Official. Many next-of-kin had not been informed of our capture; it was five months before my parents knew that I was safe, and the wife of one officer in the camp had to wait a whole year.

Christmas was a difficult time. We did have half a Red Cross parcel each to cheer us up, better meals and a Church Service. But nothing can replace home at Christmas. Yet in some ways that Christmas was the most meaningful one in my life. In the afternoon I lay on my bunk with a grumbling tummy which had an unfamiliar amount of food inside it. My mind went naturally to home and to the wonderful family Christmases of the past. Then I thought of the origin of Christmas: the birth of Jesus in a grubby stable away from home in an enemy occupied country, and soon afterwards the escape to Egypt as a refugee in danger of his life. Away from the normal festivities, as a prisoner in a foreign land, I was able to identify more fully with the birth circumstances of the Christ Child and I felt very close to Him.

Bridge was a major time consumer in camp. Nearly everyone played. I enjoyed a game when studies permitted. Sports of many kinds took place but on the advice of a British doctor, soccer matches were only played for ten minutes each way because of our undernourishment. An athletics match was held and I was highly tipped for the high jump, but only managed third. The highlight came in the Summer of 1943 when the Red Cross produced some cricket gear. We had a number of good cricketers in camp including two England players: Bill Bowes and Freddy Brown. They captained the two sides. I played without distinction. The pitch was on the main roadway through the camp and the outfield was a bit rough, but that did not detract from our enthusiasm. Initially the guards were a nuisance: they would stride on to the pitch between overs, and inspect the stumps as though they were some escape device. They were less keen once someone had taken time to explain to them that unless they stayed well behind the boundary, they were likely to get a very hard ball between the eyes. They withdrew to a safe distance and sang their arias. The details of the match appeared in the Yorkshire Evening Post some months later when the news reached Bill Bowes' wife at Pudsey.

CHAPTER 4

ESCAPE

In the bag, escape was a subject in most people's minds at some time or other, and in some people's minds all the time. Individual attempts at tunnelling or escaping in other ways were discouraged. A few brave efforts were made but without success. There was an official camp escape committee to which any escape attempt was to be submitted and, if approved by it and the Senior British Officer, the scheme could go ahead and assistance would be given. But any would-be escaper was encouraged to channel his energies into the official project.

The official camp escape scheme was similar in concept to the one made famous in the book and film: "The Wooden Horse". In our case it was a blackboard, not a vaulting horse, which disguised what was going on under the ground. Each of the four residential blocks had a courtyard at the back in which there was a well for washing water. Every fine day there would be a lecture in each courtyard. Each lecturer would have a blackboard placed at the rear of the courtyard near the well. In front of the blackboard would be a large mat covering the opening of the tunnel. The tunnel went straight down for about six feet before going along towards the perimeter wire and wall. A square wooden frame was made for the surface opening of the tunnel. Into that frame was fitted a shallow wooden box, like a seedbox, which was filled with the same sandy soil that was around the opening. This formed a lid for the entrance and when in place, with the soil smoothed over, totally concealed the tunnel. The diggers would often be left down there for several hours at a time.

One of the main difficulties with tunnelling is getting rid of the soil. In this case, with a lookout for guards by the open end of the courtyard, the mat in front of the blackboard would be moved and the lid taken off. Cardboard boxes and bags of soil would then be handed up and the dirt tipped down the well. The empty containers were returned, the lid and mat put back and the lecture continued. Our washing water would be more cloudy than usual for the next few hours.

In August 1943 the Italians surrendered and the Germans took over our camp. Three of the four tunnels were now well beyond the perimeter wall, but had not yet reached the cover of the bushes as planned. However it was decided to open up exits for those three at night and put similar box lids on them, as on the entrances. This was quickly done and, when the Germans ordered us to parade with our belongings at 9 o'clock the following morning, the tunnels were ready for use. A doctor in our number estimated that fourteen people in each tunnel would have enough air for two nights, should they be prevented from getting out the first night. I was allocated the task of putting the lid back on our tunnel when the fourteen had gone down. I just had time to rake the soil over and hurry to the parade ground as the German guards appeared.

We were taken in trucks to another camp at Sulmona in central Italy, where there was an important railway station. Obviously we would be put on a train to Germany as soon as possible. Meanwhile, we heard later, the forty-two people we had left down the three tunnels all got out the first night. Most got back to the Allied lines in the south.

Sulmona was an old camp built by the Italians in the first world war for German prisoners-of-war. It consisted of a series of brick huts with the cookhouse at the top of the sloping ground and the parade ground and German quarters at the bottom. The Germans assured us that we would be much better treated under them and they did indeed increase our food ration to two rolls a day instead of one. We knew that this would mean the Italian civilians would have even less.

In the Chieti camp, four of us had shared adjoining wooden bunks; the other three were gunners who had been captured at Tobruk. They were: Clifford Wilton, a big rugby forward of the London Scottish, George Burnett, later a distinguished banker, and Bobby Blake, now Lord Blake. The four of us stuck together in Sulmona and were joined by two more gunners, Ken Lowe and Beverley Edge. We also befriended a commando, John Craven who had recently come into the bag. When two of us were walking round the new camp, we began to plan a way of hiding up inside the camp when the Germans evacuated us. Others were also thinking up schemes as none of us was keen to go to Germany.

The seven of us agreed on a plan and went to work. From outside the hut under the eaves, it was possible to take out two lines of bricks above the ceiling line. Through this hole it was possible for a slim person to squeeze into the roof space without damaging the ceiling. With the bricks replaced, we could hide in the roof space, possibly without detection. As it was an old camp and recently pulled about when the previous prisoners had been evacuated, there was plenty of bric-a-brac lying about. We began to collect what we needed. With one of us watching out for the patrolling guards, we took out the six bricks necessary and, over the next few days, put up what we could: wooden planks on top of the rafters to provide enough floor space for us to lie on, blankets, tins of water and whatever food we could spare or scrounge. Then we made a cat-walk of planks to an earth box in one corner of the roof to be our toilet. We had barely completed this operation when one midday we were unexpectedly summoned for a roll-call. This must be it!

The five of us hurried outside and up through the hole with our few belongings. Then Clifford and our commando friend, whose frames were too large to get through the hole, bricked us in and rushed off to the parade. Twenty minutes later they were back in the hut below us to collect their things and to call through the ceiling: "We're off to Germany. Best of luck!" It was September 30th, George Burnett's birthday.

It was our intention to stay in the roof as long as possible. Initially we had thought seven days would suffice. Our camp intelligence officers had forecast a rapid advance of the Allied troops up through Italy. It was known that there had been successful landings at Salerno. It was thought that the Germans had few troops in the south of Italy and they were expected to withdraw and form a defence line further north. We hoped to stay in the roof until they had gone.

Life was bearable but very uncomfortable in the roof. We had enough floor space on the planks for the five of us to lie down. During the day we propped ourselves up and, if all was quiet, moved around a little to relieve our aching limbs, but mostly we sat or lay down. In the dark we developed an acute sense of hearing to compensate for our lack of sight. I was lucky in having with me a Bible and to be immediately below a shaft of light through a crack in the tiles. I read it through twice. Within a few days we rationed ourselves to two biscuits a day with something on them and a third of a pint of rusty water each. With such a small intake of food and liquid the earth box was not needed at all after two or three days.

Our hopes of a German withdrawal began to fade. We could hear the rumble of military vehicles at night and sometimes during the day. We tried to believe it was going north but had to admit it was actually going south. The German guards thought there were more of us hiding up in the camp than there were. This was because a number had got through the wire on the first night. A few who were hiding in less well prepared places than ours were caught. One of these British officers, Wingfield-Digby, was made to come round and shout threats into each hut to anyone who might be hiding there. Sometimes he would manage to add an extra bit of information for the benefit of anyone like us who might hear. One morning he was instructed to say that every hut would be blown up the next day and that anyone hiding should give themselves up. The following morning we heard a series of single explosions getting nearer. The next hut above ours received what my gunner friends thought was a hand-grenade. Our hut was next. Bobby Blake was on watch at the spy-hole, through which he could see the entrance door and suddenly he whispered: "Duck!" as he put his hands over his head between his knees; we did the same. With relief we heard something hit the floor without exploding, it was an old shoe. A few moments later a hand-grenade went off in the next hut below ours. They seemed to be doing alternate huts.

A day or two later we thought for a while that the Germans were shelling the camp to get us out, but as we listened to the shells whining overhead, the experts with me decided that they were firing at a small monastery or hermitage on the mountainside just above the camp. We heard later that they thought there might be some partisans sheltering there.

One evening there was a buzz of excitement among us as we heard voices of Germans approaching and soon soldiers were entering our hut! The whole place resounded with noisy talk and shouting as they selected beds. The camp was being used by the Germans to house their own troops as they moved south. At night we lay as still as possible for fear of being heard; we could hear their breathing quite distinctly as they slept. I was not popular with my companions because of my tendency to wheeze and sneeze. Fortunately the German's hearing was not as acute as ours had become. As they were going to bed one night we were amazed to hear "The Lambeth Walk" coming from an old wind-up gramophone. They played it over and over again night after night. Clearly it was as popular with them as was "Lili Marlene" with the troops of the 8th Army; at our request "Lili Marlene" was played over the camp address system at Chieti every night just before lights out.

After another batch of German soldiers had been billeted below us all was quiet again. The day came when our meagre supplies of food and water were finished and we must leave the comparative security of the roof immediately. It was the night of October 19th. We waited until midnight, removed the bricks and quietly let down the long plank to the ground. One by one we slid to the ground; it was a strange sensation when my legs touched the ground: there was absolutely no strength nor feeling in them and they buckled under me. I crawled to a nearby water tap and just drank and drank and drank, then I ate half an American iron ration which we had scrounged. It was like a small piece of dark chocolate but full of vitamins. Gradually the feeling and use of my legs returned.

We divided up to make a reconnaissance of the camp, reporting back in fifteen minutes. It was decided which two places were the best for attempting to get out through gaps knocked in the perimeter wall. Beyond that was a floodlit mud road and then two lines of barbed wire with sentry boxes every forty yards or so. Edge and Lowe would attempt to get out of the camp on the side which was in the general direction in which we wished to go. George, Bobby and I would attempt the other side. If we got through, we would have to skirt back right round the camp to be able to set off in the right direction.

We lay by the hole in the perimeter wall, watching the guard outside his sentry box about twenty yards below us. The one above was not manned. After a time the guard went into his box. We waited and waited until all seemed to have been quiet for a reasonably long while: we hoped he was dozing. Slowly George started to crawl on his belly across the brilliantly lit road towards the wire and began to lever it up. I started to crawl towards him across the road and Bobby followed once I had reached the wire. In turn each of us held up the wire for the other to crawl underneath and eventually we were all three outside: it had taken an hour. What a moment of great relief and exhilaration, but we could not stay and enjoy it; we must put as much distance as possible between the camp and ourselves before daylight. We began to make our way up and round the top of the camp; the going was steep and rough, over rocks and scree, and we seemed to make a good deal of noise. Two hours later we were the other side and a short distance from the camp. Utterly exhausted, we lay in the shelter of a bush and slept.

I was woken abruptly by the sound of heavy boots scrunching on the scree and coming up the slope toward us. I could hear German voices. We held our breath and they went past us up the hill. We wondered: were they a search party out looking for us or merely a working party going to cut down some trees? Years later we learned from Edge and Lowe, who were caught, that it had indeed been a search party! It was now quite light and the first glint of the sun was glistening in the dew drops on the leaves. The sheer beauty of the scene after all those months of baked mud in the camp, with no vegetation in sight, made me feel that, even if we were re-captured, it would have been worth getting out just to have seen again for those few moments, the beauty of God's creations. Once the sound of the boots had died away we discussed what we should do next.

I was very blessed in my companions: George was a major, and the senior among us; he was a natural leader and a man of balanced judgement. Bobby had picked up a good deal of the Italian language with his keen retentive mind. I could do little except pray. We decided we must press on. Fortunately, to start with, there were a number of bushes to afford us a little cover. After a while the vegetation ceased as we continued to climb up and across a bare spur of the lower slopes of Mt Morrone. We felt very exposed to any prying eyes from the peasant farms and smallholdings where German soldiers might be billeted. Before midday we were exhausted again and rested in a gulley on the mountain slope. I had my first painful bowel movement for seventeen days. In a further discussion it was agreed that we must take the risk of going down among the houses in the valley to find food and water, and hopefully somewhere to rest up for a while to regain our strength. So after our rest, we began to make our way diagonally down the slope, still heading in a generally southerly direction. Some time later we were passing within a quarter of a mile of a country dwelling near which two or three German soldiers were working on a military vehicle. A group of Italian children were looking on and we could see them quite clearly as they spotted us and attracted the attention of the Germans. Fortunately they took no notice and carried on mending their truck, while we hurried on.

A little later we came to a clump of trees and Bobby fainted from exhaustion. At the same time George and I caught sight of a peasant woman bringing her goat to a small house and George ran forward to seek her help. I kept an eye on him and also on Bobby who was soon on his feet again and hurrying to bring his better Italian to help the situation. The woman was petrified and she repeated:

"Tedeschi! Tedeschi! Germans are all around!" However, with George and Bobby explaining that we were desperate, she gave us a drink of milk out of large bowl and told us to go and hide in a ruined building nearby. Her husband would bring us some food at midnight, but we must promise to be well away before daylight.

Her husband was as good as her word and brought us a small sack of food at midnight: bread, cheese, fruit and water. He again emphasised that we must leave well before daylight and we promised to go at 2 a.m. It was so uncomfortable trying to lie on the broken rubble that we were not sorry to go.

It was late October and the night was dark. I was delegated to lead for the first half-hour. The dangers of Germans all around us had been so emphasised by the couple that, quite irrationally, I was fearful of mines, booby-traps or sleeping Germans at every step I took. The other two followed me but when it was the turn of one of them to take over, he tried it for five minutes and then complained that he could see nothing in the dark and that I had better take the lead again. We were walking along the valley and when dawn came we could see that we were crossing highly cultivated ground and that some of the obstacles we had negotiated with care were nothing more than the high ridges which divided the plots and along which the workers walked. As the daylight increased we found some tiny plum tomatoes left on dry plants and they were deliciously sweet. I had a twinge of conscience taking them, although they had obviously been left as worthless.

It was time to find a hiding place for the day. We came to a stream, drank and washed our hands and faces; it would be good to stay near the stream and the only possible place was behind a ridge dividing one field from the next: we slumped down behind it and dozed. Before long we heard someone approaching along the path on top of the ridge, we lay still. A man stopped and looked down on us; he was a big, rough-looking Italian with dark patches where his teeth had been, a man of few words. Bobby and George explained who we were and our need of food and rest. He grunted and said his wife would bring us some food and he continued walking along the ridge.

A little later we were conscious of another man looking down on us.

He was smaller and very talkative, in American-English. He told us his name was Antonio and explained he had spent many years in the United States until he had made enough money to return and buy himself a small farm. He again emphasised that we were surrounded by Germans, who frequently came to his house. When we explained that we must rest up and regain our strength, he said that in the field behind us there was a small shelter where we could spend the day, coming out only at night to wash and drink. Meanwhile, he would go and get us some food. He was soon back carrying a bottle of chianti, and with him came his wife and daughter with lamb (or goat?) chops, bread and fruit. On seeing us the good lady exclaimed: "Madonna! Madonna! Questi poveri genti!" we must indeed have looked "poor people!," emaciated and pale, with red-rimmed eyes, and of course unshaven after nineteen days in the dark roof. This family, like others we met, was so warm-hearted and generous, as they risked their lives on our behalf; we who were their former enemies. Soon we were toasting each others health and the end of the war in their chianti. We were to see our host almost daily during the next fortnight or so when he came to pass the time of day and bring us food. He would also tell us any news he had but it was usually depressing. The allies were making but slow progress up through Italy.

On the first morning, half-an-hour after our new friends had left us, another visitor came along the path. She stood before us; a tall middle-aged woman with a clear skin and cheerful sparkling eyes. She was neatly and cleanly dressed, with a bundle wrapped in a dazzling white linen cloth on her head. She introduced herself as the wife of the first man who had been along early that morning. She was as well groomed as he was scruffy. She had a beautiful bundle of goodies for us. Although we were feeling full from our earlier food, we had to make a show of ravenously enjoying her offering as long as she remained with us. As soon as she left, we put it aside for later. That evening we washed and examined our little shelter of maize stalks leant against each other to make the equivalent of a small ridge tent. The three of us could just lie down alongside each other with my feet and Bobby's sticking out slightly through the opening. Although we could often hear German voices coming across the countryside, the shelter provided an adequate resting place for us to regain our health and strength. We would come out only as dusk fell, and take a little exercise and have a wash.

In the second week of November the weather began to break. It became cooler with occasional rain, and snow appeared on the vast range of broken mountains which separated us from the part of Italy where our troops were held up. Our host agreed that we needed a good guide to get us through the Maiella Range of the Appenines. Up to now we had not been strong enough to go, we had been hoping that our troops might do the crossing for us, but with the approach of winter we also needed better accommodation.

The matter was settled for us by the sudden appearance of Mario, a bumptious but adventurous eighteen-year-old youth. He had heard on the grapevine of three English officers hiding in the countryside and had searched until he found us. He offered to shelter us in his mother's flat in Sulmona. He promised to return the next day with a meal, to demonstrate his good faith, and make the necessary plans. This gave us a chance of checking up with our host on the trustworthiness of Mario. So it was that a few days later George, Bobby and Mario led the way across country followed at a distance of a few hundred yards by Mario's uncle and myself, into the busy streets of Sulmona, bristling with German troops. As well as praying, I remember whistling "Lili Marlene" to keep up my spirits. We arrived safely at the second floor flat in a large block near the town centre, the house of Signora di Cesare where we were to spend two interesting months.

CHAPTER 5

THE WOLF OF THE MOUNTAINS

Signora di Cesare was quite a well-built lady, with a large heart and plenty of courage. She had been widowed for many years; her husband, we were told by Mario, had been a general. The sister-in-law, who lived with her, was a small nervy creature, as excitable as Signora di Cesare was calm. Mario took after his mother in build but little else, he was boastful, bumptious and, at times, rude.The flat consisted of a fairly spacious living room with a charcoal cooker, kitchen sink, chairs and table. There was a small toilet at one end near the entrance door and a big bedroom off to one side. A large window looked out onto the street.

In the bedroom was a great matrimonial bed plus a small single bed. At night the three of us would retire first and occupy the big bed, leaving a space for Mario who would arrive later, after his youthful escapades. When the three of us were settled, we would call out: a hand would appear to turn off the light and then the two ladies would creep into the single bed in their slips. In the morning we would hear the Signora rise very early and go off to search for food. Sometimes she came back from the fields with some turnip tops, they tasted rather like spinach when cooked. At first the three of us took it in turns to sleep next to Mario, but before long it was decided, by two to one, that my catarrh was so bad I could not possibly be as offended by his smell as they were, so I had to sleep next to him every night from then on!

Life settled into something of a routine in the di Cesare household. I still had my Bible with me and went aside after breakfast (ersatz coffee and sometimes a small piece of bread) to say morning prayer, and again in late afternoon to say evening prayer, which I could remember off by heart. Not having a lectionary I made out my own scheme of Bible readings and psalms for study. As I lay in bed at night, I would say as much of Compline as I could remember. I got two lines of the Compline hymn slightly wrong and to this day I tend to sing or say it that way.

Life could be boring in the flat all day, though occasionally it could suddenly become all too exciting. The cry would resound through the town: "Rastrellamento!" The Germans were having a roundup of Italian men, usually to take them in trucks to the front to dig trenches for two days, after which they would drive them back to the town square and push them out totally exhausted.

Two British officers hiding in another part of the town were caught one day and were dropped back after their two days of labour. On the warning cry of "Rastrellamento!", our routine was to go along the corridor to the central stairway and climb to the top of the building through a trapdoor in the ceiling, into a roof space which seemed to stretch endlessly above a whole line of buildings. We met many interesting characters up there while waiting for the all-clear.

Although contact was made with some other escaped prisoners hiding up in the town, we thought it safer to lie low rather than meet with them. This decision was made after two British army officers had turned up at our door one day with two Italian women. They had escaped from Sulmona hospital where they had been sent by the Germans for some illness before the camp was evacuated. They were now living in another part of the town. After they had gone, Signora di Cesare was rather upset, she said that the Italians were "fallen women." So, for our hostess's sake, as well as our own, we sent a message on the grapevine to the effect that we would not return the visit and would be glad if they did not come again or tell anyone where we were. The good sense of this decision was seen some weeks later, at New Year.

Apart from the occasional "Rastrellamento", life was rather monotonous sitting all day in the one room looking out of the window. To relieve the boredom Mario suggested he should take George out with him one night and Bobby on another, for a drink in a nearby bar. My Italian was not good enough to risk taking me. When George went, he and Mario started to play a kind of billiards; before long, a German came to the table and looked on; Mario, in his impulsive way, challenged him to a game. George was furious but could only comply: they made a foursome with one of Mario's friends. As there was only one cue, when George had finished his shot, he had to pass it on to the German. His fear was only surpassed by his anger with Mario and no more evening trips to the bar were made.

Food was scarce; the Italians had been rationed as early as 1936 and had never received their full rations. They showed us their old ration-books which were full of unused coupons to prove this. Most foods and other needs came through the black market. When we arrived at the di Cesare's there was a live hen in the flat, it was intended for the celebration of the arrival of the Allies but this bird had long since been killed and eaten. As Christmas drew nearer and food scarcer, the di Cesares opened up a secret room. Behind a bookcase in the living room, another small room had been boarded up: it contained some stores of flour and wine for emergencies. It was amazing how quickly word got round and family and neighbours were calling in for a drink. There was even a visit by the carabinieri, who had heard that the di Cesares were harbouring some prisoners of war. Of course they did not want to do as they should and tell the Germans, especially if a little wine was forthcoming! We were brought in from the bedroom to join them in a drink.

One day, just as we were finishing lunch in the flat, there was the unmistakable heavy tread of German boots coming along the corridor. We fled into the toilet as the loud knock came at the door: we could hear five of them talking to Signora di Cesare and they stayed a long time. Eventually, and with great relief, we heard them leave. I am not quite sure what it was all about but it gave us a scare. We were very glad none of them wanted to spend a penny!

On Christmas Eve the Signora went out very early in the morning to scour the countryside for something special to eat. She came back about midday triumphant: she had procured half a sheep's head. The church bells were ringing that evening more than usual in their nondescript jangle. The aunt went to mass and we looked forward to Christmas lunch, although with some reservations about the sheep's head. Signora di Cesare was busy that morning making a more substantial pasta than usual, gnocchi and boiling her half sheep's head. There was still a little wine left from the secret room. We three were each offered in turn the eye of the sheep before Mario eagerly crunched it up! A bit of the sheep's cheek was more to our taste. We thought of home, our parents of course had no idea where we were nor of how we were spending Christmas.

Early on the morning of New Year's Eve, Mario came in with the news of a rumour that the Germans were going to raid houses where escaped prisoners were staying, that night. Hasty arrangements were made for us to go to the neighbours; the Black Beetles we called them, because they were small, round and very dark. They had a sort of love-hate relationship with the di Cesares. It was from the Black Beetles that we learned of Mario's fraternisation with the Germans at the railway station where he worked, inviting some back to his flat and getting his mother to do their washing. When the Black Beetles got on to Mario about this, threatening to report him to the British when they arrived, Mario decided he needed something to put him in favour with the British. It was for this reason he had sought us out in the fields.

But to return to New Year's Eve: in the evening we were escorted across to the Black Beetle's flat and in due course to bed in the bridal bedroom. It was a good-sized room, garishly furnished with a huge posh bed awaiting the marriage of the first black beetle to take place. The privilege of sleeping in this bed was offset by the fact that it was riddled with bed-bugs; those small red crab-like creatures which come out in the dark and dig their teeth into any human flesh they can get at. We had been spared these in the di Cesare household. We experienced no raid that night, but heard what had happened later.

The two officers who had called on us and who lived in another part of the town, had continued to befriend an Italian woman they had met in Sulmona hospital where she had been as a result of British bombing. Just before Christmas, the woman had decided to reap the benefits of the rewards of food and money that the Germans offered for information about escaped prisoners of war. She had given the address of these two and their three friends who lived nearby. The Germans had carefully planned their raid to pick them up at midnight of New Year's Eve. They drew a blank. An escaped Scot had found rather good accommodation on the other side of Sulmona and had sent a message to the five desiring their company to celebrate Hogmanay. Defying the curfew, the five with the aid of Italian friends had made their way to the Scot's lodgings and proceeded to celebrate. While doing so, news was brought of the raid, so in the early hours they made their way to the station and caught the milk train to Rome, which the allies liberated four months later.

After the New Year excitements life returned to routine. Snow began to fall in the town. Food became very short again and we were conscious that we were becoming a burden, not that the Signora would say so. The Allied troops were unlikely to appear until the Spring, but what chance had we of getting over the Maiella mountains? The deadlock was broken for us. Mario came bursting in full of excitement just as we were finishing breakfast one morning. Alberto, a mountain shepherd, known locally as "The Wolf of the Mountains," was assembling a party to go over the mountains into the British lines. He had already taken two parties through in recent months. He was to take a third that night: would we like to go? We asked questions, especially about Alberto and whether we could trust him. We sent a message back by Mario to say we were interested and would let him know definitely by early afternoon. The snow was now really thick and it needed a frost hard enough to enable us to walk on top of the snow.

After Mario had departed, I went into the bedroom to say a morning prayer and to pray for direction. The psalm I had set for that morning was 121:
"I will lift up mine eyes unto the hill.
    From whence cometh my help?
My help cometh even from the Lord."
When I went back to the living room, I told the other two about the psalm and that I was ready to go. We agreed that we should risk it and told Mario at lunchtime. During that afternoon Mario brought the news that the expedition was postponed for 24 hours for lack of frost. Late the next morning Mario came in to say that the expedition was almost certainly on that evening, and we had to rendez-vous with Alberto and the rest by six o'clock at a certain spot outside the town, to which Mario would escort us.

I said evening prayer early that afternoon. The psalm set was 91, which includes the words:
"He shall give his angels charge over you,
    to guard you in all your ways.
in their hands they will bear you up
    lest you dash your foot against a stone."
There was a lot in that psalm to encourage us in our venture. Some time after five-thirty p.m. we said our farewells with heartfelt thanks from us and tears from the ladies, and we left with Mario, down the stairs and out into the snow of the deserted street. We looked up and waved to the weeping women at the open window. I threw two snowballs at them to try and cheer them up.

That was the last I saw of Signora di Cesare for fifteen and a half years. On a camping holiday across Europe with my wife and children, I finally located her, now living in Aquilla with her married daughter, whom I had never met. When the daughter let us in and opened the flat door, Signora di Cesare looked up, recognised me, put aside her knitting and came across the living room exclaiming:

"Arturo!" She gave me a great bear hug then she stood back and scolded me for not writing more often, with tears of delight streaming down her face. She greeted my family and then, with her daughter's help, busied herself borrowing things from neighbours and laying on a great feast; the sort she would have loved to have given us all those years ago in Sulmona, but could not. I felt very ashamed of the small present we had brought with us from Coventry Cathedral. This fine, courageous woman, who had been a mother to me for those two months, risking her life daily for us, deserved so much more than I was able to give her.

With Mario the three of us reached the rendez-vous just as it was getting dark. The moon was not yet up. The snow was thick. Most of the others were already there; more would be joining us a little way up the mountain. Some were escaped prisoners, most were Italians who wanted to get into the safety of the British lines for various reasons. We were about 20 altogether; Alberto addressed us briefly, urging us to keep together and follow the track he set for our safety. He was a stocky man with a weatherbeaten face. As we were to discover, he was a man of action but few words; more like a Yorkshire or Northumberland shepherd than the talkative Italian men I had met so far. He set off at a cracking pace into the increasing darkness. We were soon climbing into the foothills, and then ever higher and higher. The moon came out and then a little further up where we passed below a lip of overhanging snow, there was some frightening howling. Standing on top of the overhang, silhouetted against the moon, was a leader wolf with his pack behind him, not very far above us. It was a shock. I did not know that there still were wolves in Italy. I seemed to remember that they were unlikely to attack a group of people, only a single straggler. It was an added incentive to keep together.

As we got higher we could hear rushing torrents in deep ravines below. We came into an open expanse of snow and I suddenly went through the frozen crust on which we were walking and found myself up to my armpits in snow. In my exhaustion I just wanted to rest and soon began to doze off. Suddenly I came to, realising that I must not sleep or that would be the end of me. I struggled onto the surface again and tried to catch up with the rest of the group now well ahead.

By daylight we had reached the top of the 7,000 ft pass, gathered together and rested awhile in a shepherd's hut. Alberto told us we had been very slow. He had hoped to get us right through to the Allied lines in one night but we had so far only managed to get halfway there. He would go through in daylight and ask them to send out a patrol to meet us. He said he would come back and rendez-vous with us at 9 p.m., in a sheep pen he pointed out to us on the other side of the valley. He would have to be careful skirting round the valley for there were Germans in the village below. We could not spend that day in the hut as it was visited regularly by German ski patrols: we had seen their tracks; we would have to take what shelter we could in a sparse copse nearby. We lay there all day in the bitter wind; I have never been so cold: we were not dressed for such conditions and were chilled to the marrow. I think perhaps we would have been better off in the hut for outside we were easily visible. Fortunately for us no ski patrols came that day.

At about 6 p.m. we gathered in the hut to try and get warm. Some were fortunate in having a bit of food with them. One kind Italian saw how perished with cold I was and gave me a swig of "grappa", a clear liqueur: fire water. It burned my insides all the way down and then irritated my ulcer. Eventually we set off under the leadership of Francesco, a resistance fighter, round the edge of the mountain and aiming for the distant sheep pen. It was not easy to keep out of sight of the village hundreds of feet below but we arrived on time. After 9 p.m. then 10 p.m. came and went without any sign of Alberto. Francesco, George and another officer went down to the shepherd's cottage below us. They returned with dire news: Alberto had been caught by the Germans in a "Rastrellamento" in the village that morning. We decided to wait until 11 p.m. but there was still no Alberto. Many were for pushing on without him; I was praying like mad and asking for guidance. Shy though I was, I found myself strongly urging that we should give Alberto until midnight: only he knew the Maiella mountains and without him we should have poor chance of survival. One other officer supported me and finally it was agreed that we should wait until midnight. The moon came up and a few minutes before midnight we saw a lone figure come up to the shepherd's cottage below us. Francesco and the two officers went down again and quickly returned to say that it was Alberto and that he would be with us in a few minutes after a brief rest and something to eat. He had spent the day shovelling snow, clearing roads for the Germans.

At ten minutes past midnight we set off, trying to keep up with Alberto. Once we started to descend the path became covered with slush, a thaw had set in on that side of the mountains. As we made our way through the woods we heard the howling of another pack of wolves but did not see them. Later on we came upon a derelict village; I could not decide whether it had been destroyed by shellfire or simply decayed. We scavenged for food and water in the light of the moon and from the shadows a man suddenly revealed himself. He had remained hidden long enough to make sure of our identity. He was an Italian returning the way we had come with a sack of white loaves of bread procured from the Allies. In starving German-occupied Sulmona he would be able to sell them on the black market, it was a regular journey he made two or three times each week. The bread was too valuable to allow us any.

At one point Alberto suddenly doubled back; with the thaw starting the path was too boggy. From my position near the front of the group I now found myself near the rear. Well on into the night we came upon a mountain torrent in full spate, the water roaring as it tumbled down. This we would have to cross if we were ever to reach the British lines. Alberto had chosen a crossing point where there was a large rock in the middle of the torrent. He went first to demonstrate that we must first jump onto the rock and then from there to the far bank. Having been something of a long jumper at school I volunteered to go first and managed to get across safely. George, a good deal shorter, did well to get to the rock, but then his foot slipped and he was in the water. Fortunately the brave Francesco had already waded out into the river and he stood below the rock for just such a contingency. With the water swirling round his chest, he caught George before he could be swept downstream. The same thing happened to one or two more of our party before we were all safely on the other side. Alberto set off immediately, anxious to get as near our lines as possible in darkness. By 9.30 a.m. we were straggling into an advanced position of the Royal West Kents who were based near Casoli. Later we heard that both sides had had their guns trained on us as they wondered who and what we might be.

As each of us passed a certain gate, an officer of the Royal West Kents was checking us in with Alberto, who wished to make sure of his 100 lire for each British prisoner of war. I tried to express my thanks to him but he just grunted and I was again reminded of Yorkshire shepherds. I expressed my heartfelt thanks aloud to Almighty God and, privately, in my heart, told Him that I wanted to let Him guide every day of my life from now on in the way He had guided us safely over the mountains to freedom.

CHAPTER 6

ROMANCE AND MARRIAGE

The troopship docked at Liverpool early one morning. As I disembarked, I was met by two R.A.F. Police who conducted me to London by train and then to the Air Ministry. I was debriefed, granted leave and given a rail warrant home. On the way to Paddington I got the taxi to call at Simpson's where I bought an officer's greatcoat to cover up my tattered clothing including my homemade sack trousers. In the train home I was conscious of the other passengers looking at my feet, on which I had a pair of army plimsolls with slits cut into them to relieve the swellings on my feet.

It was like a dream arriving back at the big Warwickshire vicarage of Hatton after two years. I was brought back to reality with a jolt when I saw how much older my parents looked, and I hoped I did not show my shock. Four sons in the thick of the war in far-flung places, as well as a house full of evacuees, had taken their toll. In addition, my father was an air-raid warden and always up when Coventry and Birmingham were being raided; my mother was billeting officer. There were no flags out for my homecoming and I soon settled into the routine of filling the oil lamps, sawing wood and pumping up the water into the tank. There were a few shy looks in my direction in church on Sunday, and the milkman left a carton of cream with the farmer's compliments.

I had forgotten how beautiful England was. My homecoming coincided with winter just beginning to give way to spring with its fresh green. The form and colour of the first crocus in the garden rooted me to the spot for several minutes as I gazed at it in wonder.

On the troopship I had fallen completely for a most attractive, petite E.N.S.A. actress, later to become a film star. On board we were inseparable. A week or so later I went to London to see her and go to a show but I came to earth with a bump. She was sophisticated and used to the very best, I was a poor country bumpkin and it showed!

Pat, a vivacious brunette, of whom I had become very fond just before leaving England, came to stay for a few days on my return home. We were still very fond of one another, but a lot had happened in two years and I had changed probably far more than she had. I felt God would give me a definite go-ahead when I met the right life partner and I did not get a clear green light. She returned to her first love, an army officer, and married him.

I used part of my leave to go and visit some of the officer's wives whose husbands had gone to Germany from Chieti and Sulmona, starting with the lovely wife of Clifford Wilson, who had bricked us up in the roof. Another I went to see was Bill Bowes' wife and that was how the details of the Chieti cricket match found their way into Yorkshire. The wives were all very grateful to get some first-hand news of their husbands.

After a while I was posted to R.A.F. Shawbury to do an Advanced Navigation Course. One day some high ranking R.A.F. officer was visiting the station and we had to parade for hours. I found I was still subject to my earlier tendency to faint and I went down with a bang. Apart from that I did well on the course and was one of two to finish with a distinction. I was also invited to become a Fellow of the Royal Meteorological Society as a result of my 95% in the Meteorological examination. Because of these results I was posted to R.A.F. Llandwrog in North Wales to be in charge of Navigational Training there. My work consisted mainly in the organisation of lectures and timetables for the Officers and Senior N.C.O's who were already there and doing their jobs very well without my assistance. However, one thing I did introduce was a Swear Box, each word costing threepence, thus benefiting the Red Cross. Initially they did very well but eventually the income reduced until one day an officer came in, put half-a-crown into the swear box and really let fly.

At my first breakfast in the Mess I collected my scrambled eggs from the hatch together with my egg-cup full of sugar, the day's ration, and went to a place on a free table and got myself a cup of tea. I finished my scrambled egg and went to make myself some toast in the electric toaster on the side. When I returned to my place with my toast and another cup of tea, a tall slim W.A.A.F. officer was sitting opposite and my egg cup of sugar was gone. A very embarrassed Lettice Caldecott explained that she had thought I had finished my breakfast and so had added the sugar to her store in a screw-top jar. It was not perhaps the best of introductions but we were soon learning a good deal about one another, she having spotted me as a newcomer the night before.

The evening after the breakfast episode found us playing shove ha'penny together after dinner. She noticed the book I had with me called "God and War" and asked me if I were a Christian. She told me how she came to know Jesus as a personal friend and promised to lend me a book which she had found helpful. As I read the book during the next week or so, the main point that struck me was that to receive the blessings of the Christian life, one had to surrender oneself to Jesus one hundred per cent; I knew I had not done this. I had been conscious of God's Holy Spirit guiding me at various times in my life, not least in recent months, and I had told God that I wanted Him to guide me all the time when we had arrived safely in British lines. But when I had got back into an R.A.F. Mess I found it was not so easy. I knew I was compromising. Yes, I wanted to please God and let Him guide me some of the time. At others, as when out drinking with the boys and flirting with the girls, I wanted to direct things myself.

I finished the book one evening just before dinner. After the meal I went across in the dark winter night to the little nissen-hut chapel. I did not put the lights on but went halfway up the chapel and knelt down. I wanted to be done with compromise once and for all and to give my life totally to the Lord. I told God out loud that I gave Him my whole life totally for ever and I felt it in every part of my being. As I did this the chapel suddenly seemed to be full of the most glorious light, filling my own body also. I was conscious of the person of Jesus alongside me as a particularly brilliant light and knew that He was indeed divine. The warm glow of the Holy Spirit flowed into every part of me. I am not sure how long I remained on my knees bathing in that glowing presence, but when I left the chapel I felt about ten feet tall and seemed to be walking on air.

In the next weeks God seemed to be very much in control and began dealing with me in very practical ways, such as with my shyness. That Saturday afternoon I needed to go into the nearby town of Caernarfon. As I got into the local bus my instinct was to make for an empty double seat but the Lord said: "No, go and sit next to that man over there and talk to him. Don't worry if you blush and stumble for words. I am in control." I obeyed. On the station I began to find various people coming up to me and unburdening their troubles, not only fellow officers, but some other ranks as well.

The peak of Snowdon was clearly visible from our station and I was conscious of its having a deadening effect upon me, I suppose like claustrophobia. It was, I thought, like the mountains that had penned us in for so long and which had prevented us from getting to our troops, and also the hill that towered oppressively over our camp at Chieti. As a result of prayer about this, the first Saturday we both had free, Letty and I took a train and walked up Snowdon. It was no longer a threat after that.

My friendship with Letty and our love for one another developed swiftly. Letty had received many proposals of marriage, but, like me, had always felt that God would let her know when she met the right person. We both quickly felt that God was saying: "Yes!" However, the formal engagement did not come until a few weeks later when, on a Saturday off, we took a train to Colwyn Bay and bought a nice second-hand gold ring with a single diamond. After a meal we went back on the train to Caernarfon and there, on a frosty winter's night, huddled up in our greatcoats on a bench seat below Caernarfon Castle, I formally proposed and after her acceptance, put the ring on her finger.

Letty's mother had died when Letty was born and her father had died of a heart attack at the beginning of the war, in their home at Bournemouth where Letty was looking after him. So I did not have to go and ask permission from her parents for her hand, but I was anxious to take Letty home and for my parents to approve. I had written long letters home telling them about her and about our proposed visit on a certain weekend. Either they could not read the letter or had put it aside halfway through. After all, with four boys my mother and father saw many girls come and go. We travelled overnight on Friday to make the most of the time, arriving at the local station of Hatton in the early hours. A walk of a mile and a half by road and fields got us to the huge old vicarage at 4.30 a.m. and we found the doors locked! I tried the windows and found the kitchen open. With some effort we climbed into the warmest room in the house: it had an Aga-type stove that usually stayed in through the night. We were drinking our second cup of tea when my mother came down in her nightdress to stoke the stove and make the early morning tea. She professed ignorance of our coming and later told me that she knew nothing about Letty! So much for my long illegible letters. Fortunately I did not tell her there and then that we were already engaged. She gave Letty a warm welcome, as she did everybody, and my future wife was amazed at the wonderful meals my mother put before us on that large kitchen table, all produced on a paraffin-oil stove and the Aga. We had no gas or electricity and the water had to be pumped. My handsome seaman brother was home on leave and he teased Letty unmercifully, saying how sorry he felt for me. It was not long before it had the desired effect of an explosion from Letty. It was as well that my two other brothers were overseas.

We had planned to marry on Easter Monday 1945, but my parents persuaded us to wait until May 19th, Whit Saturday. It was just as well that we agreed to this delay as Letty was very spotty with measles at Easter. V.E. Day came shortly before the wedding and threatened to sabotage arrangements because we were warned that our leave might be cancelled. The authorities seemed to fear that airmen might desert as soon as the war finished in Europe and all officers would be needed to prevent this happening. However, we were able to go ahead as planned except that only one plane-load of friends was able to fly down from Llandwrog and they were mainly the heavy drinkers rather than the others we would have preferred.

It was a lovely service: Bobby and George from Sulmona days were both able to be there. The village ladies laid on a marvellous lunch in the Village Hall, including a salmon from one of the flight sergeants in my section, whose father had some fishing on the Tweed, and a ham from our butcher in Wales. The honeymoon began at the Mayfair in London with lobster: it was amazing the meals you could get in London during wartime if you could pay for them. The Mayfair was very good in giving lower rates for British servicemen, so one or two reunions of those who had escaped from Sulmona were held there. We went to Westminster Abbey on the Sunday and on to Porthleven in Cornwall for the second part of the honeymoon. This was a let down: the food was poor and the room cold.

Letty was not allowed back to Llandwrog once married as theoretically she was on duty twenty-four hours a day looking after the W.A.A.F. So she went to Bicester and I went to Llandwrog to begin the rundown of the navigational training courses. Later I was posted to Scotland where Letty, now out of the service, was able to join me in digs in Newton Stewart before I was posted to Northern Ireland. Then Letty, now several months pregnant, went to my home. I spent much of my time working at my Greek, a correspondence course, as I needed to pass it in order to take up my place at the Queen's College, Oxford. Our daughter, Felicity, was born on March 14th 1946. She was reluctant to come into this world and my compassionate leave from Ireland nearly ran out before she appeared. I was demobbed in the Spring of 1946, went home and took the Greek paper in Solihull Grammar School early in July. I had to wait until September for the results. I had passed and could begin at Oxford in October 1946.

CHAPTER 7

OXFORD AND WELLS

I had taken my entrance exam for the Queen's College before going into the R.A.F. with a view to reading History. Now I opted for Theology, desirous of getting as fully equipped as I could for the ministry as soon as possible. Letty and Felicity stayed with my parents at Hatton vicarage, while I went to a college hostel for the first two terms, under the care of my scout Joe Blackadder, later to become the Head Servant of the College. It was reassuring that the college porter and the librarian both remembered my father and grandfather; the latter had been a Fellow. Nevertheless, I felt like a new boy and my inferiority complex reasserted itself. I had a great need to prove myself.

I found the academic work hard and made it harder still by wanting each essay to be a masterpiece. Three times I worked right through the night trying to perfect an essay for the next day, before seeing in prayer that this was wrong and due to pride. I decided that in future, if I needed to finish an essay, I would set my alarm for early in the morning and do it then. A year or so later I had become more relaxed about my essays and, if time was pressing, would do as others did: copy large chunks from books on the subject. On one such occasion, when the whole of second part of the essay was copied direct from a certain author, as I was reading it to my tutor, he went to his bookshelf, took down the appropriate volume and followed the essay in it. When I had finished reading, he simply said: "I should not depend quite so much on that author in future!"

It was accepted that we play games every afternoon and that suited me. I was soon playing hockey for the College and later, cricket. In my second term I also got into the University Athletics Team. I travelled by train from Oxford up to the White City with a very young medical student, Roger Bannister. We were both rather shy and nervous. As we chatted, he told me that he was to be eighteen the next day and his father had promised him a tracksuit for his birthday if he won. That afternoon, against Cambridge, he came first in his event, the mile. I came last in mine, the pole-vault. Probably realising that I was feeling low, Harold Abrahams, of Chariots of Fire fame, was very kind to me that night at the formal dinner.

After two terms I managed to get a semi-detached house on an estate in Botley, where Letty and Felicity joined me. I had bought a 1934 Morris 10 in 1940 and now it came into service again. Botley was too far out to be convenient so we stayed there only one term. In the long vacation we suddenly got a telegram from Professor R.H. Lightfoot offering us a flat in very centre of Oxford, adjacent to, and the property of, the Oxford Union. We wired acceptance. The eminent professor was most impressed by our efforts at redecorating the flat and as a token of our thanks I did some redecoration of *his* flat. He was most concerned that we had nowhere to walk Felicity in her pram and eventually got permission for Letty to take her to the Fellows' garden at New College, but Letty never felt bold enough to take him up on his offer. In any case, Felicity seemed to enjoy the hustle and bustle of the High and Carfax.

Before long, Letty's granny, in her late eighties, came to join us in the flat, her bedroom doubling up as my study. Apart from that, there was our bedroom, a living room and a kitchen, which also housed the bath and the mice; all on two floors above a tailor's shop. Granny's physical strength was not matched mentally. She had been living with a succession of companions, who could not take her foibles for long and so they had left. After a while I had to sympathise with them. She and our 18-month-old daughter were of an age mentally, and would get into heated arguments which would degenerate into:

"Did!", *"Didn't!"*, "Did!", *"Didn't!"* for ages; or else it would be: "Naughty Felicity!", *"Naughty Granny!"* "Naughty Felicity!", *"Naughty Granny!"* Granny was always losing her handbag and would accuse us of stealing it. When she did find it again, usually under the pillow on her bed, she would carefully count the money within, apparently quite a large sum, to make sure none was missing. On one occasion she came down in the morning with hat and coat on, carrying her handbag and umbrella and said: "Will you get me a cab? I'm going to see my mother." She became physically, as well as verbally abusive when Letty and I tried to explain to her that her mother was in a place which could not be reached by taxi.

We did a lot of entertaining in that flat so conveniently placed at the centre of Oxford. Folk were always popping in for a chat and a cup of tea. Saturday afternoon was "Open House" for anyone who would like to come to tea. Then we had a fellowship evening on Sunday. Granny loved these occasions as everyone made a fuss of her and made sure she had plenty to eat and drink. She remarked to one person: "I know Arthur and Letty find it quite hard to make ends meet but they have a good idea: they run a cafeteria. But I never see anyone paying." All this did not make the flat the most conducive place in which to study, but I could, and sometimes did, go to the Union Library next door and work there.

Liberal Theology was firmly established and in the ascendancy. It was difficult not to be affected by it, expounded as it was by such clever people. Looking back I wonder whether they were not more in love with their clever ideas than they were with God, and sometimes confused the two. Letty, who would have loved to go to the University herself to read history, decided she would accept second best and read my essays. She soon gave up when it seemed that nothing in the Bible was what it said it was. It seemed that I was studying a God who was speculative, whose miracles could be rationalised and whose book, the Bible, was solely an object to be criticised. Not that I think we should approach the Bible in a gullible way, but with respect and humility, realising that we are dealing with truths that are ultimately beyond human understanding.

My tutor was the Rev. Dennis Nineham, chaplain of the Queen's College and a little younger than myself. For a year I overlapped with his star pupil, David Jenkins, later to become the Bishop of Durham. I can remember Dennis recommending to us both a new book called, I think, "The Birth of Christianity" by Duschene. It included a brilliant debunking of the literal resurrection of Jesus. I was shaken and turned to other authors, like Ramsay for his little book on the Resurrection. After further reading, thought and prayer, my belief in the literal resurrection of Jesus was strengthened and has been unshakeable ever since. But, nevertheless, for years I approached the Bible with critical scepticism.

I was kept in touch with the living God of action by remembering my experiences of Him during the war, and through my recent association with the Oxford Group or MRA, as it had become known. Their faith was real and practical. A group of us met in our flat at 1.30 p.m. each weekday lunchtime. We would exchange news, share any special thought from our early morning "quiet time", which each of us had, and pray, before dashing off to our 2.30 p.m. games. On Sunday evenings after Church, we had a longer time of fellowship when more of the "Town" were able to join the "Gown", including a future Lord Mayor. He and his wife, Bob and Mary Knight, were a wonderful socialist couple, who had dedicated their lives to the service of the community. We also befriended some of the Africans, many of whom had been won over to communism.

After one of our lunchtime gatherings, two of us dashed off to play hockey for our college against the full University side. For them it was a warm-up game in preparation for their match against Cambridge in a few weeks time. Perhaps it was the prayer beforehand, but our College side excelled themselves and beat the University 6-0. I had a blinder, playing in goal, and was elected a member of the Oxford Occasionals. I had several games with them, one with Bobby Blake, with whom I had escaped, who was now a student at Christchurch. I was also asked to play cricket once for the Oxford Authentics, but did not have a good game.

At some point I met two very tall Fijian princes who were studying at Oxford: Mara, who later became Prime Minister of Fiji, and his cousin Edward who later became Minister of State. I got to know Mara well: he was a most outstanding man. We often high jumped for Oxford University in various matches, with me very much the second string.

An interesting tale was told of Edward. He was invited by one of his college friends to come and stay at his home in the lowlands of Scotland and play in the Lairds' XI against the local side. For the occasion he wore the traditional Fiji sports dress of a kind of white skirt, which looked not unlike a kilt. Over the tea interval, the local reporter was interviewing Edward and asked him:

"Have you any Scottish blood in you?" and Edward replied:

"Well, you could say I am Scottish by absorption. You see, my grandfather ate a scottish missionary." Over twenty years later I was telling this tale in Chedworth vicarage to a group of about a dozen Fijians. They were students at the nearby Royal Agricultural College and a few of them were staying with us. We had invited some more of their fellow countrymen for a pleasant dinner on Christmas Eve, before they sang at the midnight service. As I finished the story, there was a burst of laughter and one or two of them said:"It's absolutely true, and the missionary's name was Donald MacKenzie."

My Finals at Oxford drew alarmingly near. At the beginning of my penultimate term I had *Collections*, which consisted of an old exam paper in my subject; I was appalled as I read through the paper, I hardly knew what they were talking about. I could not answer a single question and returned a blank paper. The shock made me get down to revision in earnest. My parents offered to have Granny for the last two months before my finals. When the time came, prayer and trust in God helped a great deal, especially while waiting for each paper and during one night when I could not sleep at all because my brain was so worked up. I passed, but only with a third.

I opted for Wells Theological College. It was a broad based college, neither extremely high nor extremely low church. I had tried both wings of churchmanship at Oxford and had not been very happy with either. At both extremes there seemed to be a tendency towards bigotry: an attitude of "We are the only true Christians".

The two years at Wells were more restful than those at Oxford. It was a lovely city for the family to live in. We were fortunate to rent a large Georgian house in the Close from the Dean and Chapter; later it became the Deanery but was then vacant. The Chapter Clerk was most helpful and we shared the house with another couple. During our stay there, both wives produced their second child within a few weeks of each other. Ours was a boy, John. Felicity was then nearly four. I had to live in College for the first two terms and again for the last term. The majority of us had been through the war.

The daily routine consisted of monastic-like services interspersed with intellectual lectures. Wednesday and Saturday afternoons were free for games, mainly cricket and hockey. On another afternoon we did some practise visiting at the geriatric hospital or at one of the outlying villages. I did most of mine up on the Mendips at a little village called Emborough. The villagers looked forward to our visits and would tell how they had been visited by

Archbishop Fisher when he was a student. On Sunday evenings we might practise taking a service or preaching a sermon, which was sometimes pulled to pieces later in the week by fellow students and staff.

There was plenty of fun, theological leg-pulling and mimicking of the cathedral staff. There was some complaining, either about the irrelevance of much of what we were doing to the world outside, or more often about the freezing temperature in the Lady Chapel of the Cathedral where we said our first office very early in the morning, sometimes followed by a period of meditation. I did not find the bitter cold conducive to godly thoughts.

John Robinson, later to hit the headlines in various ways when Bishop of Woolwich, was Chaplain at the College and one of the lecturers. He was often provocative, but seldom dull. One remark of his has always stayed with me: "The level of normal living for a Christian is above the miracle line." I did very well in my general ordination exam and those over me were surprised that I had not done better at Oxford.

CHAPTER 8

EARLY YEARS IN A DOG COLLAR

Iwas made Deacon in Southwark Cathedral on St Thomas's Day, 21st December 1950, aged 30, and ordained Priest a year later. After attempting to go to the East End of London for my first curacy, I ended up at Horley in Surrey, where there was a lively church and two daughter churches. Letty and I were fortunate to have a caring and wise vicar and his wife, Jack and Priscilla Torrens, who knew Jesus to be alive and active today. We threw ourselves into parish work with great zeal, convinced that the world could be won for Christ within a few years. We all ended up ill!

At the beginning of my second Lent I had glandular fever, then 'flu in Holy Week, preaching at the Good Friday three-hour service with aspirins and a glass of water in the pulpit. On Easter Monday I led the Youth Fellowship for a 20 mile hike across the Sussex Downs. On the Tuesday I took the family for a few day's break to Bournemouth. That night, in the hotel, I had such a raging fever that Letty sent for a doctor first thing in the morning. I went to hospital for six weeks with pneumonia and pleurisy. There I experienced the great benefit of penicillin. Letty meanwhile, was developing gallstones and our daughter Felicity, who had inherited my asthma and bronchitis, had such a bad chest that the doctor said that only six months in Switzerland would help her. By a series of miracles, three months became possible and she returned wonderfully better. Finally, our lively son John went down with severe glandular fever. The stagnant water, that was later discovered beneath our small house had not helped.

During our time at Horley we experienced the full range of parish activities, their snags and their joys. We learned something of the cost of caring for the needy. One tormented soul, a man in his forties, turned up regularly at our back door. He engaged us, especially Letty, in long involved discussions getting nowhere; eventually we discovered he was a serious schizophrenic. He often had a meal with us and for a while slept in the garden shed as our small house was overflowing with family. We were very conscious of our inability to help this man. We were also conscious of the limitations of medical science and the social services in such cases. Letty and I have a great admiration for our doctors and for the medical profession generally. We have reason to be very grateful for all the help that we, as a family, have received from them over the years. But in cases like this man and others, more was needed than medical know-how or human care, even when motivated by the love of God.

We were sincere in our desire to help and care for people, and to extend God's kingdom of love. We sought God's will and prayed earnestly for people. We asked God to bless what we were doing in His name and He often did so. But, by and large, we were serving Him in our own strength, rather than relaxing in His sovereignty and allowing His Spirit to work through us. We had not yet learned to seek and use constructively the gifts of the Holy Spirit. This took many years and we are still learning. Nevertheless, we did begin to get glimpses of the power of Jesus to heal through His Spirit.

One day I noticed in the local paper that a 12 year old boy, I will call him George, had been awarded the Scout Cornwall Award for his great bravery throughout numerous operations. He had fluid coming from his brain in such quantities that they could not control it, even with a draining tube down the back of his neck. There was nothing more the hospital could do and he had been sent home with only a few weeks to live. I asked the vicar if we had any contact with the family. We had not, but he thought it would be a good idea if I visited them.

They lived in a private housing estate on the edge of the parish. With some trepidation I rang the bell. The chatty blond mother let me in and led me through the hall to the sitting room. I did not know what to expect but there on a bed to one side of the room, was a deathly pale face in a grotesquely large pear-shaped head propped up slightly on a pillow, for George was paralysed. My first reaction was one of revulsion which I hoped did not show. My second reaction was a strong and a strange one: almost of anger against the disease. I said to myself with great depth of feeling: "Jesus doesn't want this." The mother explained to George that I had come to see him and left us alone for a while. She had something to do in the kitchen.

I asked George if he knew Jesus. He knew nothing about Jesus. I told him very briefly of our Lord's life on earth and of his death and resurrection for us. I told George how He helped and healed people and that I believed Jesus wanted to help him. My mind went back to an article I had read on Christian healing a few years previously, I think it was by Agnes Sanford. When George's mother came back I told her that I believed Jesus wanted to help her son. If she would like to think about it and teach George the Lord's Prayer, I would come back in a few days and pray with him and ask Jesus to help him. His mother said she would like that and I left. I wanted time to think and pray about it myself: my faith was slight.

A few days later I rang to confirm my visit and went round. I did not feel any more confident or full of faith than before, but very nervous. I just hung onto the conviction that God did not want the boy to suffer like that. I had not found "Prayers for the Sick" particularly helpful or relevant and had concocted a prayer of my own. I went in and talked to George a little more about Jesus. George was unable to talk or respond very much but he showed interest and a desire to know more. I read one of the stories of healing in the Gospels, diffidently prayed my prayer laying on my hands on his head, said the Lord's Prayer with him and pronounced the blessing. I made a date to come back to see him in a week's time.

To my amazement, on that visit, I found him sitting up and looking cheerful. His head had stopped swelling and had begun to go down. We talked further about Jesus. I prayed with laying on of hands again, thanking God for the improvement. I continued to visit George and minister to him. Before I left that parish a few months later he was walking around, his head almost back to normal. I last heard from him when he wrote to me on his 21st birthday, which he was to celebrate that evening with a party.

In spite of George's remarkable recovery, doubts and scepticism filled my mind. Had my prayers and laying on of hands in the name of Jesus anything to do with George's healing? Would he have recovered anyway? Was it just a co-incidence? Thoughts of this kind were going through my mind even before we left Horley. I had read Theology at a very critical school at Oxford University. I had been taught to question everything, especially the miraculous and supernatural. Like most people in our culture, I had taken on board the general outlook of Western Civilisation which includes a strong element of scepticism and materialism. I believe this outlook is a major hindrance to the development of the Church's Ministry of Healing. Scepticism was the main reason for my doing little more about this ministry for many years.

In 1953 we were intending to move for a second curacy to an industrial parish in Coventry with 22,000 people, where several well-known firms had their factories. This was the industrial heart of the country, I thought, which must be won for Christ if the country itself was to be won for Him. Then I went down with pneumonia and pleurisy and Bishop Neville Gorton of Coventry would not hear of our going to live opposite the gasworks and near several factory chimneys. He also made some perceptive remarks about not using my zeal for Jesus and consequent spiritual energy to drive myself into the ground. Instead of a second curacy he offered me several parishes as incumbent, one of which, when we went into the little Wren church, we immediately knew was right. This was Honiley linked with Wroxall, two country parishes. It also included the chaplaincies of Wroxall Abbey girls' boarding school and of R.A.F. Honiley which then had three squadrons. It was certainly not a rest cure but we loved it and our health improved after Letty's gallbladder was removed and Felicity got over a severe bout of glandular fever. Also we were in adjacent parishes to my old home of Hatton where my father was just retiring as vicar. It meant that I was nearby for the last two years of his life. I was able to handle the funeral arrangements when he suddenly died and to support my mother with whom I became much closer.

It was a scattered country area with the two churches and the R.A.F. station chapel. We enjoyed it all including the girls' school about which I had felt somewhat apprehensive, thinking perhaps of St Trinian's. But once I started coaching the girls' cricket, I felt more at home. There was a new doctor just starting up a country practice, he was a churchman who enjoyed singing in the choir and bell ringing and he proved to be open to the ideas I was beginning to take on board from Agnes Sanford's book, "Healing Light". We saw that our jobs as doctor and priest often overlapped and we worked closely together. I often referred someone to him and he often referred one of his patients to me as we met on our rounds. I can think today of several people who benefited from our co-operation. But still I only prayed for the sick; I did not have the faith to offer them the laying on of hands for healing in the name of Jesus, until the next crisis.

A lovely family lived several miles from the church in the middle of nowhere, but worshipped regularly at Honiley. He was a self-employed forester and his attractive young wife used to work hard with him out in the open air whenever her duties of mother and housewife would allow. She became ill one winter and assuming it was the 'flu, she soldiered on. But it proved to be meningitis and eventually she was rushed into intensive care. I was rung up that Saturday evening and told it was touch and go whether she would live through the night. How we prayed and pleaded with God that night and in the services the next day. She held her own and slowly improved but was left with T.B. in all the joints of her body. She was transferred to a sanatorium a few miles away where she lay flat on her back in a plaster jacket. I felt however that God did not want her to be an invalid for the rest of her life. I spoke to her about the possibility of Jesus healing today as he had done during his earthly life. At the same time I did not want to raise expectations that might not be met. Although I knew God had the power to raise her from her bed and heal her instantly, yet I did not believe that was what God would do in her case. I did believe he would hasten and complete her healing as she co-operated with the doctors. I offered her the laying on of hands in Jesus' name and prayed along these lines. I visited and ministered to her every week. Sometimes I took a Christian filmstrip or some slides to project on the walls for the courageous folk in that ward. Wanting to use her time constructively, she did some embroidery for the church, working at a frame above her head as she lay flat on her back. In due time, a lovely pulpit fall was dedicated and used regularly in Honiley church.

Slowly though it seemed, she did make a remarkable and complete recovery and went back to working with her husband. She even surprised her doctors by giving birth to another lovely baby. A few years ago I was invited back to preach at Harvest Festival at Honiley and there she was with her husband, looking as fit and young as ever.

My scepticism again made me ask myself whether my ministry had made any difference or whether she would have recovered as quickly and fully anyway. Physically I had no means of telling, but certainly in other ways she was greatly helped. On one of my early visits she said to me:

"I thank my God every day for this illness, for through it I have learned so much that I never would have learned had life jogged on normally." I knew what she meant from my own early years of illness.

Honiley was really only a hamlet with a church, a pub, the estate of Honiley Hall and the airfield. Yet thanks to a very able young leader, John Harrison, it boasted an excellent Youth Fellowship which met weekly in the wooden hut which served as a village hall. Membership was over one hundred young people coming from other hamlets and villages for miles around.

One year John Harrison went to a conference where he met a youth leader from Denmark. They arranged for an exchange. The next Summer twenty-five Danish youngsters descended on our village and were billeted in a variety of homes from little cottages with a loo down the garden, to large manor-type dwellings. Bicycles had been borrowed for them, but a local coach proprietor, on reading of the proposed visit in the local paper, supplied a coach to take them to Stratford-upon-Avon, and to Kenilworth and Warwick Castles. The following year, twenty of our young people set off for a return visit. After a long overnight journey we arrived the following afternoon at Odense railway station to be met by a decorated float on which we were taken, led by the band, to the town hall to be welcomed by the Mayor and allocated our accommodation. The homes were mostly small and modern, and impeccably kept. Some of the items of food were a bit of a shock to our country youngsters, but the generosity of our hosts defeated even their large appetites.

Bicycles had been arranged for us, but all with fixed gears, so that when you stopped pedalling, the bike pulled up with such a jolt, you were likely to fly over the handlebars. After various hilarious, if painful, incidents the first morning, cars and coaches had to be organised. Language was a difficulty at times, but there was no doubting the warmth of the friendship between our hosts and even the toughest of our youngsters. There were tears on both sides when we left for our second week in Copenhagen.

There we camped out in the basement of empty youth premises. It was not nearly so enjoyable, lacking the personal interchange. Even the Tivoli Gardens could not make up for the missing warmth of the Odense people. Letty and I were enjoying a snack in one of the romantic arbours of Tivoli when John Harrison wearily flopped down beside us saying:

"What wouldn't I give for a nice strong cup of tea and some baked beans on toast!" Within two days we were able to stop for some fish and chips on the way home!

The Honiley Youth Group compiled an excellent log of our visit to Denmark and twelve of them were invited to tea with Princess Marguerite of Denmark at her boarding school in England to present her with a copy.

Nearer to home, we organised an exchange between a group of our parishioners and a group from one of the newest housing estates in Coventry. The worshippers there had just moved from a Wimpey wooden hut to one of the first Basil Spence churches for their services. For the Coventry folk it was a little like a visit back to the middle ages. For our people it was like a glimpse into the next century. But it was beneficial to both parties as we talked over our particular problems and how our faith in Christ could help.

One day in 1958 I had a letter out of the blue offering me the Parish of Atherstone in North Warwickshire. It was a coal mining centre as well as an old market town of over 6,500 people. There were also a number of hat, knitwear and shoe factories. We went over as a family to have a good look round the town, the church and the vicarage. As we were leaving in our small car, I said to the family in general: "Well, what do you think?" One after another said we ought to go. I said I was a bit apprehensive with all those factories and people and very large church. Felicity, aged 12 immediately responded: "Daddy, you ought to know by now that God will give you the strength." So we went.

It was rumbustious, very hard work, but most rewarding. Letty and I were often up by 5.30 a.m. and not in bed before 11 p.m. The parish and community life became increasingly busy and the vicarage fuller and fuller of those needing accommodation: teachers, mining engineers and students. There was also a lorry driver, his wife and baby from the Gorbals district of Glasgow, whose room overlooked the drive up to the front door. The raucous language, clearly audible to parishioners coming to the vicarage, was anything but parsonical.

Within the first few weeks in Atherstone I made a point of going round most of the factories and down two of the coal mines nearest the town. I felt a little like a fish out of water but was able to learn a little of the conditions under which most of my parishioners worked. Getting round all the pubs and clubs took a little longer: one of the most important was The Miners' Welfare Club and the members were fiercely insistent about my having a drink every time I called. My tomato juices or bitter lemons tended to get lined up in front of me while they downed up to seventeen pints with great ease.

When the people had left the church after Evensong on my first Sunday, the thick-set ex-miner verger came into the vestry. As we put the offertory plate on the table he said:

"You'll do." I was to learn that this was high praise indeed. Two or three Sundays later I preached a little longer than usual. This time, as he came into the vestry, he loudly declared: "It's no good. they won't stand for it: twenty-two minutes. Far too long!"

My second Sunday was the first Sunday of the month and the verger told me to be at the church for 3 p.m. for Baptisms. I duly turned up and found people giving the verger names and details as they came in. It was apparently the custom for anyone wishing to have a baby baptised, just to turn up at 3 p.m. on a first Sunday and the baby would be "done." There were thirteen that day and once one started to cry the rest joined in. Afterwards I had a talk with the verger about preparation and giving notice of baptisms in advance.

Weddings could come in numbers too; I had seven one Saturday. They came in the South door and went out by the West, with the next couple already waiting by the South door. As we were just off the A.5 Watling Street, traffic could be heavy. One wedding party, who were badly held up by traffic, had to miss their turn as I went on with the next. I enjoyed weddings and had some lovely preparation sessions with several couples together for four or five weeks.

I married one old couple at 8 a.m. on a Saturday morning because they didn't want too much limelight. She was 84 and a widow. He was a bachelor of 77 who had been lodging with her for some years. He had the shakes, like Parkinson's disease, and his heart was suspect. We had to postpone the date once as he got a heart flutter from the excitement as the wedding approached. She had been, for many years, a domestic help in the household of

Canon Crawley-Boevey and his wife in the nearby village of Grendon. The Canon and his wife, both in their eighties, had retired to Atherstone and lived in a large house near the church with their three daughters. Canon Crawley-Boevey was giving the bride away and also acting as best man; the matron of honour was the district nurse. I cut the service to a minimum and allowed them to sit in the front pew for most of it. I had just started the service when the bride called in a piercing voice to the matron of honour:

"Annie, my 'earing aid!" The district nurse came forward and did the necessary and we proceeded more or less without further hitches, including the signing of the register, which I had on the spot to save their walking. As the newly-weds prepared to leave, Mrs Crawley-Boevey suddenly said: "We must have some music." She shuffled off to the nearby harmonium, used for choir practices, and played "Onward Christian Soldiers, marching as to war!" as the happy couple tottered down the aisle to the waiting taxi (from the undertakers), which was to take them to the station en route for Blackpool.

Funerals too, were numerous: I had four one day. Again a sense of humour was often needed, and also the ability to keep a straight face. Going from the church to the public cemetery or the crematorium, I use to ride in the hearse next to the undertaker: a wonderful local character. As he drove along, looking very solemn, and with people standing silently along the street doffing their hats, he would be telling me the most hilarious experiences of his long life in the profession. I would have the greatest difficulty not to laugh. In their Coronation Street type houses the family would always have the corpse lying in state in the coffin in the front room. It was one of the rare occasions that the room was used. When I called I was always expected to go and see the deceased. On one occasion the widow of about sixty solemnly drew back the cloth covering her late husband's face, saying:

"I never seen him look better in his life."

The funeral would always be followed by a high tea. My digestion still needed watching but I was usually all right if I didn't eat between meals. But I would normally go along after a funeral, if I could, for a cup of tea while firmly refusing the food, especially on the occasions that I was pressed to have a slice of lovely fruit cake with: "You must have some of this, it was made by Fanny the day she died!"

Another local custom for funerals, was to have a whip-round in the street for floral tributes to outdo the ones from the next street the previous week. Elaborate floral tributes were created: a chair made of flowers representing "the Vacant Chair,"or a gothic arch made of flowers symbolising the Gate of Heaven. The huge Parish Church was just off the town square and factory girls in their curlers and other well-wishers would crowd round the pathway to the church for a wedding or a funeral. Occasionally I was able to persuade some of them to come in. Once, when an old lag had died and his coffin was being carried in, there were no less than seven floral "Gates of Heaven" adorning the top of the coffin. An old boozing pal standing by the path said: "It will take more than those to get him into Heaven!"

Soon after I had arrived I gave notice that the Confirmation Classes would start on a certain date and at a certain time. I went along to the church hall and there were over thirty youngsters sitting in rows; apart from two in the choir whom I recognised, I knew nothing of any of them and even after a week or two I was getting no response from them. It was the worst kind of classroom relationship. For several weeks I prayed and prayed. Then in my morning prayer and intercession in church early one morning, it came to me. If they were adults, I would be taking them away for a weekend residential conference so that we could get to know each other and develop relationships. Why not have a camp? There were snags. I had never camped before. The confirmation was booked for soon after Easter, so the weather would not be suitable. It would have to be after the Confirmation in Whit week; but where? After more prayer and various suggestions, the obvious place was at our remote cottage on the banks of the Wye river, down a farm track and across two fields. I would have to hire camping equipment and another minibus to accompany my caravette. Who to help? More prayer: a name came. I had seen her in church a few times. She helped part-time in her husband's jeweller and watchmaker's shop where she served at the toy counter. I went in and she was there. I said to her:

"God suggested to me that you might help at a camp for the Confirmation candidates." Her mouth dropped. I quickly told her my ideas and told her not to give a reply now but to pray about it and I would pop in for her answer next week. When I called back she agreed and said her husband would help too. Bert and Dorothy Pickering were marvellous. So was that camp, the first of twenty-seven post-confirmation camps I was to run.

Dorothy went on to help us start a branch of the G.F.S. She was quite brilliant with those girls and prepared twelve of them for the Duke of Edinburgh Award at Gold Standard which eleven of them received at Buckingham Palace; the most ever from one club at one time.

We gradually built up some fine youth organisations, church and secular, for all ages. I often got my helpers from adult confirmation classes. One year there were twenty-five adults confirmed at once, the most Bishop Bardsley had confirmed from one church at one time. People were very diffident to help initially and I would say:

"Just come along and watch." Then I would get him or her to collect subscriptions as the youngsters arrived, and to help with the refreshments. They were soon taking more responsibility and some of the most diffident initially, proved to be excellent youth leaders.

After about a year it was decided to open the Church Youth Club, which had been in existence when I arrived, to non-church-goers. The present members were almost entirely from the Grammar School. Opening up the Club would mean, in effect, letting in the Teddy-boy Gang, most of whom had left school and were working. We had to introduce one or two new rules, such as "No coshes, bicycle chains, razors or knives are allowed in the Club", and we had to have a large man on the door to enforce it. After a month or two they stopped trying it on. The Police Inspector helped occasionally at the Club, and he and I set up a bursary fund to send youth on "Outward Bound Courses". I was surprised and delighted to see the original Grammar School lads coping better than the larger teddy-boys. The vandalism in the town soon dropped dramatically.

Within a year to fifteen months, a tall, lanky, red-haired lad was elected chairman. His way of leading a meeting was rather different from his predecessor, but he was a natural leader and did well. He had been one of the leaders of the teddy-boys. Another red-head, a very burly lad with a quick temper but a warm heart, drew alongside me on an evening walk when there was no-one else in earshot: "What's this confirmation business?" he asked "my gran says I ought to be confirmed." He was confirmed about a year later.

Another evening, some of those tough lads arrived at the Club after work, just too late for the bus which had left for the Birmingham Ice Rink. "Well!" I said to them, "I've got to go back to the vicarage as I am expecting one or two important long distance calls, but you can come and play cricket on the vicarage lawn if you want to." "Will you show us how to play?" they asked.

"Certainly" I replied, marvelling that they did not know. I found that they had never been taught at school, but were eager to learn. Several showed real promise and were soon playing for local teams.

One of the great regrets was that when I left Atherstone I had to withdraw from a great adventure. I was to take our caravette (our only family vehicle and used as a parish bus) with a County Youth Officer, tents and equipment to Italy. We were to set up camp for twenty of the older youth, who were to follow and spend a month building the first storey of an orphanage. Each youth, as well as getting time off work, had to raise £1,000 to cover his own costs and towards the building work. They earned much of the money by washing cars on Saturdays and in the evenings. The following year they went back to complete the second storey, but I was not with them as I was in another parish.

We were a male dominated church and society at Atherstone. There were over a hundred men in our branch of The Church of England Mens' Society. Once a year, it was quite an experience to hear seven or eight hundred men at the area service, giving full voice to some martial hymn in our huge church, complemented by one of Bishop Bardsley's rousing sermons.

The choir consisted of twenty boys and nearly as many men, under a great character, Cyril the organist. He also produced the annual Gilbert and Sullivan opera. He often played in church as though he were playing the Pirates of Penzance. On Good Friday night we would have the Messiah or another cantata sung by a large choir, supplemented by the other denominations and one or two imported soloists.

The Parochial Church Council consisted mainly of men. Sometimes I sensed that they regarded it rather like a trade union meeting, having a go at the boss, in this case the Vicar. But the meetings were not dull and if you sold them an idea they would have a go at it with enthusiasm; such as stewardship, street wardens in every street, house groups, parish communion to replace the dwindling matins, and a central altar, movable so that we could use the full extension of the church for big occasions. We also had a United Sunday School Campaign with other churches; two visitors from different denominations knocking at doors and inviting those children who did not attend, to come to one of the Sunday Schools in the town. Ours, which had transferred from the afternoon to the morning, to dovetail into the Parish Eucharist, leapt from 50 to over 150. We also organised a self-help scheme. A blue cardboard fish was distributed to every house in the town. Anyone in need of help could put the fish in the window and the officer in that street would call and find out what the need was and get in touch with the co-ordinator if unable to deal with it himself. On one occasion the mother of three children was suddenly rushed into hospital and the co-ordinator was able to find a woman who moved in for several weeks to look after the family.

The community might have seemed and to some extent was, male dominated, but the women were equally vigorous and forceful, and often large. Annually we had a massive fete in the grounds of Atherstone Hall, then owned by a rather delightful, but eccentric old lady living in one room. This fete had everything, including a full-scale fashion show, organised by the main ladies' shop in the town. My wife was one of those who modelled.

In saying my usual thanks at the end of the afternoon, I failed to mention one of our stalwart men, who, although he did not have an official position on the committee, did a large amount of the work. I apologised to him in church the next morning, to which he responded: "You wait until you see my missus". His missus was one of the large ladies with a voice to match. When she laughed the whole busy town could hear it. I thought I had better take the bull by the horns so to speak, and went round to her house the next morning, knocking on the back door and walking in, as was my normal practice. Fortunately I had closed the door before she looked up from her washing and realised who it was. Immediately there flooded out of her mouth at full pitch, a stream of invective, outdoing any of the men in strength and ferocity. Objectively it was quite magnificent. Feeling the size of a mouse, I was praying what to do and say. At her first pause for breath, I got in a "Sorry!" before she was off again. I prayed. A thought came, and at her next pause, I managed to get in: "I'd love a cup of tea." This deflated her a little. "Well!" she said before going on again at half volume. If the town had not already known of my gaffe of the previous Saturday, it would do by now. But her heart matched her size and by the time we had finished our cup of tea, now sitting down, we were friends again. This was just as well as this lady had an important part in the local women's dramatic efforts.

Letty had got together a number of women into a sort of concert party. One of the star turns was this very large, but not very tall lady, dressed in a tiny frilly ballerina skirt, partnered by my slim wife, dressed as the man in a comic ballet turn. The stage bounced up and down with their antics, particularly as it was only on trestles. The whole show was hilariously funny, if it was not taken seriously, as unfortunately it was, by one old people's club. This concert party had a lot of fun itself and gave a great deal of entertainment to local clubs and miners welfares in the area and often further afield. On one occasion they went to a Cheshire Home. As the Book of Proverbs 17.42 says: "Being cheerful keeps you healthy. It is slow death to be gloomy all the time."

I was amazed at the energy of these women. Most of them got up early and worked hard all day in the factories, where some of their work was physically strenuous, as in moulding the felt hats. They would go home and get the meal for the family and then off again for the evening activities. They would throw themselves whole-heartedly into whatever it was, maybe dancing, acting or a party.

I have always been very competitive and fairly successful at party games. I more than met my match in those ladies. I remember one when, on a given signal, we had to dive into the middle of the hall to get a bit of paper with a clue on it. I managed to extract a piece of paper the first two times, by the third the game had hotted up and I eventually emerged from under the pile of large women, very dishevelled, battered and bruised and without a clue! On another occasion we had to parade with our partners round the edge of the hall to music. Every so often there would be a pair of parallel chalked lines on the floor representing a river, over which the man was to carry the woman. If the music stopped when you were halfway across the river, you were out. When we got to the first river, I looked at my partner, a very large lady and shook my head. Although I was over six foot tall and fairly strong, there was no way in which I could carry her. Nothing daunted, she swept me up in her arms as though I had been a baby and carried me across, and continued to do so at every "river" we came to, much to the amusement of all.

Letty and I also had wider commitments as well as the parish. She became president of the Girls' Friendly Society for the Diocese. We both served on various Diocesan committees. I captained the Clergy Cricket XI and was secretary of the Diocesan Missionary Council. We were both involved from the beginning, with the new Coventry Cathedral, Letty as a Steward and I as a Chaplain, preaching there several times. A few of our parishioners were also stewards. It was a privilege to be at the great Service of Consecration, attended by both Archbishops, the Queen and many other dignitaries.

Of course, we also had our children to look after. Felicity was away much of the time, having been given a bursary to stay on at Wroxall Abbey as a boarder. John was at the North Street Junior School and headed up the toughest gang of boys of his age in town. They often came home with him to the vicarage, to play war games in the garden, with piercing shrieks and loud bangs; the vicarage windows were in permanent need of repair. Neither did peace descend after John had gone to bed, as the various organisations then began to arrive to use different rooms, including our bedroom a few times. Sometimes a rehearsal was also going on in the large hall, interrupted occasionally by lodgers going to their rooms.

We poured our time and energies into the community of Atherstone, where we sought to promote harmony and reconcile any factions. My sermons were sometimes on this theme. With both local newspapers sending reporters to the vicarage each Monday morning, there was an opportunity for the message to go to a wider audience. One of the reporters, a Christian, often took my sermon notes away to make an article out of them later. Sometimes a point from a sermon on Sunday would be quoted in a meeting of the Rural District Council during the week.

On one occasion we laid on a supper party for twenty trade union leaders and their wives to hear a Christian Trade Union speaker from London. The lively and friendly discussion went on until the early hours of the morning. One or two of the men were on the early shift and would therefore get little or no sleep. Two worked in Coventry factories, two others had not been to the vicarage since the Great Strike, when they came on alternate days to the vicarage and the Salvation Army for the soup kitchens.

Nearly all the main denominations were present in the town. We encouraged the Roman Catholic priest and other ministers and pastors to come to lunch at the vicarage once a quarter to enable us to work together better in our care for the people of the town. We were able to undertake a number of joint ventures as a result.

We saw at Atherstone that the Church can still play a vital role in helping a community towards wholeness. The busier we became, the more important it was to be disciplined about our morning quiet time. It often meant getting up very early, but during our Bible reading and prayer, God would often give a key thought for a person we were to meet that day or for a meeting I was to chair. St Francis de Sales says that every Christian needs at least half-an-hour with God first thing each morning unless he has a particularly busy day ahead; then he needs a full hour. We can vouch for the truth of that: we needed a full hour most days. During the challenge of these very busy days, 2 Corinthians 12.9 continued to be very important for me:

"My grace is all you need, for my power is greatest when you are weak." (G.N.B.)

CHAPTER 9

THE COTSWOLDS

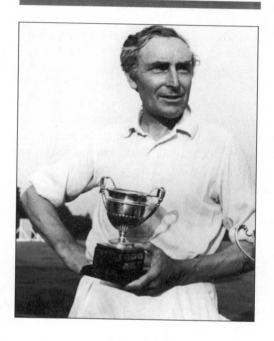

We arrived in Chedworth near Cirencester in Gloucestershire on April Fool's Day in 1964, in sleet and a biting wind. Again we took a small cut in salary, but we had an impelling call from God to go there. The invitation had come when we had reached a stage in Atherstone where all the initial aims had been met, and a church life was strong, with plenty of lay leadership. It was a possible time for a move; if we were to stay, it would have to be for another five years to see other objectives achieved. Anyway we were in great need of a day off, so a drive into the Cotswolds to have an unofficial look round would be a good plan, especially as it was pleasant October weather. However, when we returned home, we could see no point at all in burying ourselves in the valley of Chedworth. I wrote to that effect to my old college in Oxford which had offered me the living. The

Bursar rang to ask me if I would I go over again, and at least meet the church wardens, just to show that the College were doing something about trying to find someone. We took another day off, had a lovely pheasant lunch with the squire and his wife, but again said: "No!" The College persisted and asked us to go up and have lunch; I hadn't been back there since I left in 1948, and so we went to Oxford, very much enjoyed our visit, but still said, "No!"

"Don't give me your final decision now" said the Bursar, "think about it and let me know in a fortnight's time".

I did keep it in my morning prayers without any change of heart until just before the fortnight was up, when suddenly, early one morning in Church when I was not really thinking about it, the Lord said:

"Would you go to a desert island with just two people on it if I asked you?"

"Yes, Lord" I replied.

"Why won't you go to Chedworth?" I realised I had been thinking in worldly terms, of numbers and importance. Then the words of the hymn came into my mind: "God moves in a mysterious way, his wonders to perform, The bud may have a bitter taste, but sweet will be the flower." So we went, after seeing the Bursar, the Bishop, and so on.

The institution service was a bit of a shock to the quiet village as two busloads from Atherstone arrived late with some folk coming straight from work. The church was already full and the service in progress. The Bishop of Gloucester suggested that those with seats should pass hassocks into the aisles for the new arrivals to sit on. At the bunfight afterwards the polite Chedworth people hadn't made up their minds which sandwiches to have, before all the plates were swept clean by hungry Atherstonians, who then expected someone to strike up the Hokey-Cokey.

Chedworth was a complete contrast to Atherstone and it took me a year to adjust and even longer to see why God had brought us there. But perhaps it is good to stop occasionally and wait upon God. We certainly had not realised how tired we were. However, the beauty, peace and stillness of the Cotswolds quickly refreshed us and there was plenty to do, with a huge garden and vicarage. Often, after an evening meeting ending about 10 p.m., I would put in two hours of decorating. The main downstairs rooms had been decorated for us, but there were still vast areas of wall in the upstairs bedrooms and in the passages. When we got to the attics, having run out of money, we got some old wallpaper pattern books and used the pieces in them to create some interesting designs.

One of the first people I was taken to meet in the village was a real local, Reg Coates. His surname went back to Elizabethan times in the Chedworth church register. His lovely Gloucestershire burr had taken all those years to perfect. He said:

"I'm not much of a church goer, but if you'll play cricket for Chedworth, I'll come to church." We both kept to our bargain. He had been captain of the Chedworth Cricket XI for thirty years, and after another year persuaded me to take over. The great outing each year was to play against Birmingham City Police at Edgbaston. It was a merry load of passengers who came home late on the local Harvey's coach, driven by the best batsman of us all, who would never play (or drink) in that match in case injury prevented him from getting us home. And I had five services to take the next day!

One of the great delights of my early years at Chedworth was that I was able to play much more cricket than for some years, both for the village and for the Gloucester Clergy, which I captained for several years. The best standard of cricket in which I ever played was during my days at Honiley when I played for Leamington Spa in whose side were always one or two ex-county players. Fortunately for me, they were in need of an opening bowler when I arrived and I went straight into the side. We often began the season by playing the full county side and I was thrilled one year to get one of their opening batsmen with my third ball. We finished the season playing the Cross Arrows at Lords. But for sheer fun, I enjoyed both the Clergy and Chedworth games on lovely Gloucestershire pitches; few, if any, were better than Chedworth. My first summer I was fortunate to get a century, to the delight of Chedworth who had not had one for several years. A little later in the season I was very near another though I did not realise it. When I was 97, Reg Coates, the captain, came in at the other end, he played out a maiden over and then declared. I think he didn't want me to get a swollen head!

A year or two later we were playing a nearby rival village. Reg Coates, who had by then handed over the captaincy to me, was umpiring. I was having a good day with a ball that was swinging, I ended up with eight wickets. Reg was umpiring my end. Usually he was hard on my appeals and seemed to delight in saying loud and clear: "Not out!" to my "Howzzat?"

This day he was being more generous, when the opposition's number seven went back to the pavilion for a duck, the fourth to be out lbw, he said as he passed by me: "It's easy to see who's side the Lord is on". To which mid-off, nearby, added in a gruff Gloucestershire voice:

"That's the first time I've heard Reg called the Lord!" On another occasion Reg was sitting on a bench by Chedworth pavilion watching the cricket when a stranger came onto the ground asking for the vicar. Reg answerd: "That's 'im, with the pads on. Going out ter bat. You wait a minute, I expect 'e'll soon be back!"

There must have been more in our conversation on the cricket field than humorous banter, because four of the players joined a confirmation class of eleven adults. They were big, burly fellows and sat in the front pew at the confirmation service, dwarfing the small figure of the Bishop of Gloucester. Bishop Guy, who, as a fanatical cricketer, did not mind.

My greatest feat with the ball happened years later when I was in my mid fifties. I took the last five wickets in a six ball over against Bourton-on-the-Water, ending up with eight wickets altogether.

Reg and another great sporting character, Ron Jones, often came with me in my caravette to support our clergy side. They were as delighted as we were the year we got into the final and won the Church Times Cup. One of our young clergymen was shortly leaving Gloucestershire and going into the Navy as a chaplain. On the coach going up to London, Reg, who was playing cards at the back, called out to the young man: "When do you go?" The young priest replied quick as a flash: "Every morning before breakfast!" Reg dissolved into loud guffaws. When Reg died of cancer at the end of my time at Chedworth, it was a great privilege to fulfil his wish and scatter his ashes on Chedworth Cricket Ground where we had shared so many happy hours.

The first of many students from the Royal Agricultural College at Cirencester who came to lodge with us was David King. He had done well at Seale-Hayne and was studying for the Advanced Diploma in Farm Management. He became fond of our daughter Felicity and she of him. Felicity was studying at the Cheltenham Art College where she had been directed into Fashion Design, like her mother before her. Felicity had always been sorry for, and championed, any underdog. Letty and I feared that one day she would bring home a fifty year old drop-out and want to marry him out of pity. We could hardly believe our good fortune when she fell for this very square agricultural student, especially as the main contender for her affections was another David, also at the Agricultural College. After he had finished at the College and got a job, David King and Felicity were married in Chedworth Church on her 21st birthday, 14th March 1967. Lord Vestey kindly let us hold the reception in the ballroom of Stowell Park. He came to the Service but not to the reception, like one or two other Cotswold friends. We had thoughtlessly arranged the wedding on Cheltenham Gold Cup day! But 225 guests did sit down to lunch, including a few of our Atherstone friends.

Meanwhile our son John was at London University where he met a lovely London girl a year behind him called Judy Parish. When she had graduated, they were duly married and, after two years of teaching, they took a year off to go round the world before settling in Hampstead, near her parents and married sister. We all continue to see each other, in-laws and grand-children at Christmas, Easter, on special occasions and in Scotland in August. Letty and I are very blessed in our family.

Soon after our arrival in Chedworth, the parishes of Yanworth and Stowell on Lord Vestey's Estate were added to the benefice. I made a point of visiting every house in the three parishes within the first months of being there. Ten years later the beautiful villages of Coln Rogers and Coln St Dennis, which included Calcot, were also added. By that time I was Rural Dean of Northleach as well. It was a large area with 26 churches and a dwindling number of priests to look after them. The population of the whole deanery was less than the population of the parish of Atherstone. Small parishes are in some ways more difficult to care for than one big one. It is not easy preaching to three or four people, yet, if the population of that village is only 30 or 40, there are present in church a greater percentage than when there were 300 in Atherstone church.

I was also keen to share the Gospel and make it relevant to those outside the Church: to this end we had concerts and plays in Chedworth Church. For the third Lent we performed the Crucifixion scenes on Good Friday evening and the Resurrection scenes on Easter Sunday evening, from the York Cycle Plays. All the actors were from the three villages. Our first grand-daughter was born during the Good Friday performance and the news was phoned through to the pub next door, where most of the actors went after the play. When I arrived, having tidied up and locked the church, it was closing time but the landlord and his wife had lined up free drinks all round in celebration.

The following year we performed both the Crucifixion and Resurrection Scenes together during the evenings of Holy Week and opened them to a wider audience. People sat in that full church with tears running down their cheeks. One hunting gentleman from a nearby village, who had rather reluctantly been persuaded to come by his wife, said as he left: "Bloody good show, padre!" Even if the phraseology jarred, the sentiment was well meant. A few years later we did the far more ambitious performance of Piers Ploughman, in the field that sloped up from the church behind the manor, with tiers of seats especially erected. There was a long interval for all the visitors to enjoy the medieval booths of crafts and excellent refreshments in the manor yard and stables, accompanied by a fiddler. The Lord blessed us with fine weather those September evenings. We were fortunate in having in the village, Rosemary Bourne as the Producer, a hard taskmaster but a very talented lady.

I also held a Harvest Festival Service and a Carol Service in the local pub and anything else that could bring the spiritual and the secular together, short of the spiritual becoming secular! It was through serving behind the bar in the pub that I got into the National Press. This was not a gimmick but a normal act of neighbourly care. Stan and Cynthia Townsend, who ran the pub, were our nearest neighbours and good friends: neither had good health. They would not take a holiday, but occasionally would take a day off if I looked after the lunchtime session and started off the evening session until they returned. I had some marvellous conversations with men who seemed more ready to speak about Christian things there than in their own homes and I learned a few new "Gates of Heaven" jokes. I also gained a good deal of knowledge about the village and its people, as was the case when I did the post round annually to let the postlady off to help her sister with lambing in Devon.

A freelance press photographer happened to call when I was serving in The Seven Tuns. He went to his car, got his camera and took one of me pulling a pint. Two days later it was in the Daily Express. Five years after that he phoned me up and asked: "Do you still serve at The Seven Tuns?"

"Occasionally" I replied, and gave him the date when I would next be there. He came and took another photograph.

"It'll be in The Sun tomorrow" he said.

"Not on page three I hope" I replied. Next morning at 8 a.m. A.T.V. Central rang up from Birmingham having seen the Sun and asked if I could be at The Seven Tuns at 12.00 noon. They arrived with cameras and half a dozen crew and I was on The News that night. They were fair in reporting what I had said. A snippet of the Gospel might have got across to someone who would not otherwise have heard it.

After about fifteen months, I had suggested a Deanery Mission to my fellow clergy. To explore this idea we had a large deanery meeting with the Archdeacon and Diocesan Missioner. It was a disastrous meeting, though good came out of it. Few laity had any idea of what was meant by a mission. We were obviously nowhere near ready for such an enterprise. Those who went to church needed to know much more about the Christian faith before they could share it. So for several years, on two or three Saturdays a year, we had a series of training days on the basics of the Christian faith. These proved very helpful both in their teaching and their fellowship. On one November Saturday two or three people even gave up their hunting! We also had an occasional day of prayer, and in Lent deanery mid-week services or study groups. One of these studied the social needs of our rural area. One practical result was the start of the first day centre for the elderly who lived on their own in the area, run by a number of volunteers. At Atherstone I had sought to build up lay leadership and delegate as much as possible. This proved more difficult in the rural areas which were still largely feudal in outlook and where the parson was expected to do everything in connection with the church.

Meanwhile, my interest in the church's ministry of healing was developing. I was more often offering the laying on of hands, when I prayed with the sick at home or in hospital, without any spectacular results, though some said it had helped. Then came a landmark: the first of several people in whom there was some visible result. Soon after the Colne Valley parishes came into my care, I was told that one of the hunting fraternity from there had had a bad riding accident and was in Cirencester hospital with a broken bone in her neck. I rang the hospital and was told I could not see her for another two days and then, when I went, the sister told me I could have only a few minutes. As usual I was rather diffident as I went into the ward where she was propped up in bed. Her good looks were spoiled by two very black eyes. After a few general remarks, conscious that the sister might return at any moment and remove me, I asked if she would like the laying on of hands with prayer for healing. She said: "Yes, please!" although later, she had no recollection of saying that, as she was heavily sedated at the time. I said a tentative prayer as I laid my hands gently on her head and then bid her farewell. She later told a friend that the acute pain in her head ceased from that moment. She was out of hospital in a few days, to everyone's surprise including mine. A month or so later she rang me up and asked if she could see me. When she was settled in the vicarage sitting room, she asked if she could have laying on of hands for pain in her back. I had a check from the Holy Spirit and suggested she read a book to help her understand what this ministry was all about. I fixed another date for her to come and see me again when she had finished it. When she returned a week or so later I asked her:

"Do you still want laying on of hands?"

"No, I want forgiveness," was her reply. After confession and absolution, I administered the laying on of hands with a prayer for the healing of her back. It was soon better. Some weeks later she came again and said:

"I think God wants me to be a healer." She tells me that I was very stern in my retort, to the effect that Jesus was the only healer. Nevertheless, she was one of the first of the laity to be involved in the ministry of healing within our group of parishes. By then she had matured a good deal in her Christian life and was disciplined in her practise of an early morning quiet time. She was one of those who had laughed when I first suggested this to her, saying she was no good in the morning. She would do her Bible reading and prayer at night. However, like others, she came to value that early morning quiet time greatly and soon found an hour was hardly long enough.

During this period, a wonderful Christian couple had been led by God to leave the London area and buy a farmhouse in a village a few miles away. They used it for Christian teaching and renewal meetings for people in the Cotswolds and beyond. I heard of strange goings-on there. When the parish had been without a rector for a while and, therefore, under my care as rural dean, I decided I had better find out for myself what was happening. I knew from past experience how wrong or exaggerated rumours can be. I rang up and they invited Letty and me to tea. We immediately took to them and Letty started to go to an evening Bible study in their house. I went whenever I could to the day seminars for clergy and lay leaders which they held about three or four times a year. I heard and met there such speakers as Colin Urquhart, David Pawson, Archbishop Bill Burnett and Bishop Morris Maddocks, among others. Later I went regularly to the course of Kingdom Faith teaching tapes by Colin Urquhart. These were most valuable times of praise, teaching, training and fellowship for two hours on a Wednesday morning, ending with an excellent ploughman's lunch. For a busy parish priest like myself they were a chance to take in and receive, rather than always to be giving out. Also they were a most valuable means of training up lay leadership, and of Christian growth for myself and many other people in the area. But meanwhile the Deanery Mission happened at last.

The Deanery Standing Committee, consisting of two priests and three lay people, was having one of its regular meetings. They were always prayerful times of fellowship as well as dealing with necessary business. In the middle of this particular meeting we were getting nowhere. We could not see where the Lord was wanting us to go. We had had our training days, increased our fellowship across the Deanery, encouraged prayer and study groups in the parishes, looked at some of the needs of the wider community, out of which had come the Day Centre, and considered a great range of minor matters. What did the Lord want us to do next to make the area more Christian? I suggested we had a period of quiet waiting upon the Holy Spirit, asking God to show us. After a few minutes of silence, a farmer's wife said:

"Maybe the time has come for the Deanery mission." All agreed. There and then I rang Bishop Cuthbert Bardsley to see if he had a free fortnight in about two years time to lead such a mission. Amazingly I got straight through to him, and after consulting his diary he said the only available gap in his commitments was in fifteen months time, in February 1978. I asked him if he would keep it free and I would confirm or not by letter. I reported back to our meeting and, although it was the minimum time necessary to prepare for such an event and the worst possible time of the year for snow in the Cotswolds, we decided the Lord was telling us to go ahead.

We threw ourselves into the preparations: producing literature, such as a Theme Leaflet, an Invitation-Programme and a Prayer Leaflet; gathered together helpers, got up sub-committees and all the other things needed for such a venture. The period of preparation, as well as the event itself, was a time of spiritual growth for all involved. Humanly we were out of our depth and so had to rely on the Holy Spirit, conscious that it was God's Mission not ours.

There were many tests of faith, much hard work, several crises and above all, a very great deal of prayer. I became more aware of being involved in spiritual warfare than ever before and learned the necessity of putting on the whole armour of God first thing every morning before going into battle (Ephesians 6.10-18). At the same time I have never been so conscious of being upheld by the prayers of others and, therefore, so at peace in a big event.

Every house in most of the parishes received an invitation, literature and, where possible, two visits. God blessed the mission greatly, not least with the weather. The whole of Northern Europe was under a blanket of snow that fortnight except for a twenty mile radius round Northleach church, which was packed for each of the four main meetings. Bishop Bardsley had insisted that there should be a personal testimony by a lay person on each evening. Three of the four had never done such a thing before. Each one was very different, but most moving, and gave a good lead-in for Bishop Bardsley, who as usual was most inspiring and challenging. Many who came, gave their lives to the Lord, were counselled and followed up, even those who were in the area but who did not come to the meetings knew the church was alive and about its business. One farmer, who came to the Lord through the mission, was to become the Deanery lay chairman a few years later. His wife was on the organising committee. She had returned home enthusiastically after the first meeting and remarked what a miracle of answered prayer it was, that we were the only area in Northern Europe not under thick snow.

"Yes!", replied the farmer, "and all the pigeons in Northern Europe are on my oil-seed rape!" A small price to pay for new life in Jesus. Among the few who came to the Mission from outside the Deanery, was another very efficient farmer and his wife, Robert and Mary Henly. Getting to know them was to bear an unexpected harvest a few years later.

As well as the follow-up groups for adults across the Deanery, we also felt led to concentrate on developing our work with young people, who had not been catered for in the Mission. An excellent course for potential Sunday School teachers, led by the diocesan children's officer, was organised. A village was often too small, with very few children in it, to have its own Sunday School, but it could combine with one or two nearby villages and have a joint one; the same happened with youth clubs. We also had our first Deanery family "Faith and Fun Day", this involved hiring a secondary school for a Saturday and inviting whole families, including some who had little contact with the church. We began with a shepherds pie lunch, then broke up into groups. The young, in their various ages, had workshops on a theme, and the adults a teaching session followed by group work. Everyone came together again for tea, followed by an informal act of worship, in which the young displayed the work they had done. The first day was near November 5th so we finished up with a bonfire and hot dogs.

Nearly a year after the mission, in January 1979, the Deanery Standing Committee was meeting in a farmhouse seeking to find where the Lord was leading us for the coming year. We were not getting very far, so I suggested a time of waiting on the Holy Spirit. After several minutes of silence, I invited the other four to share any thoughts or ideas that had come to them. Then I shared the only real thought I had had, and said:

"What about taking a Deanery party down to Lee Abbey?"

"What's Lee Abbey?" they asked

"I'm not sure", I replied. "I believe it's a sort of Christian conference centre. I know a couple in Somerset who went with a small party from their parish for a weekend and found it very beneficial. A few days down there together might further deepen our faith and fellowship." They agreed that I should investigate the idea and I wrote off to the the Warden of Lee Abbey, the Rev. John Perry, and had a most helpful letter back. We arranged to take a Deanery party down there for a Monday to Friday stay in mid-November, a good time of the year for farmers to take a break.

It was with some trepidation that sixty-six of us went down to Lee Abbey in North Devon, wondering what we had let ourselves in for. We need not have worried; it was marvellous in every way. The loving and gentle welcome by the community, mostly young people, put everyone at their ease. The house was comfortable and warm without being luxurious; the coastal scenery and surroundings were beautiful. The course of talks each morning, on themes we had suggested, were excellent. After coffee we split up for group work. The afternoons were free to explore the countryside, the evening activities were varied: always fun and very helpful. Our stay finished up with a great celebration Eucharist on Thursday evening.

One item we asked to be included in the programme was a service of

Christian Healing. Three of the incumbents in the Deanery were now involved, to some extent, in the ministry of healing and we knew that there were a number in our party who would welcome such a service and ministry. It was a memorable service and an encouragement to us to develop this ministry in our own parishes. In this and in other ways Lee Abbey continued to be a place of inspiration and refreshment to us. Each year we took a party down there in November, often joined by folk from neighbouring deaneries. One year the number rose to 115, a full house!

About this time we were asked to produce something for the Three Counties Agricultural Show in Malvern, for the following June, 1981. When I mentioned it to the Deanery Secretary, she threw up her hands in horror and said with unusual vehemence:

"Arthur, we can't take on any more!" She got my usual response: "Pray about it." I felt we should do something, as we had experienced and faced many of the problems of rural communities and sought to find some answers. There were the problems of loss of facilities in villages, such as shops, post offices, schools and buses; fewer local farm workers and more commuters and retired people; amalgamation of parishes: we had gone from thirteen priests to seven in my time. Working as a Deanery, we had brought these problems to God and found some answers. To cut a long story short, we produced, with much prayer and hard work, a fast-moving, audio-visual presentation, which was shown over and over again during the three days of the show, while visitors flocked to our tent because of the excellence of the refreshments our ladies produced. Afterwards more copies of the sound strip were made to go to other rural areas of the country. Our excellent bookstall also provoked a good many questions about the Christian life.

My wife is a very sociable person and fond of entertaining. She was always badgering me for a free evening. The only evening which was normally free of engagements was Sunday, unless I had an adult confirmation class on the go. So, after church on Sunday evening we often had people in to a meal to meet each other and for us to get to know them better. Letty could not always remember whom she had asked as she plodded round the village; she didn't drive. It usually worked out all right. In the early years, an invitation went to each family in Yanworth and Stowell with our Christmas card, to a party just after the festival. Sixty or seventy would turn up for eats and party games including charades, murder and sometimes sardines, in the big old vicarage. The Head-forester and Head-housekeeper demonstrated surprising talents.

When we first arrived in Chedworth the population was very static. Some locals had never ventured further than Cirencester, and that rarely. The village had been entirely self-supporting with its butcher and baker, shop and post-office, pubs and two bands. Anything else was brought round by the carter from the station, including fish on Fridays. Increasingly this changed and, during our time, more and more residents came in from outside. One way we sought to blend in the newcomers was to invite them to the vicarage for a party. Several times a year we would have one on a Sunday evening, or occasionally on a Saturday for the benefit of weekenders. Letty was often one of the first to call on a newcomer and would immediately ask them to our next big get-together. We would also ask some of the more established members of our congregation to come and welcome those who had recently arrived. Numbers were a bit of a guess, but it was usually between 30 and 40, which we could just manage for a buffet supper in our new vicarage. Letty made a curry and rice, I boiled a ham, one or two friends brought a pudding and the evening looked after itself, more or less. There was the famous time when Letty brought together two people she didn't recognise, saying:

"Do you know each other?" He replied:

"We ought to, we've been married for thirty years!"

Many people said how much this welcome to the village had meant to them. Some, who had not been in the habit of going to church where they had lived previously, started to come regularly.

In the late summer of 1981, for once, I failed to drop straight off to sleep one night. So I prayed and then asked God if there was something He wanted to tell me. He gave me two clear thoughts: one was that we should invite a team up from Lee Abbey for a week of events in the Cotswolds, where we now had this developing Christian fellowship across a wide area of three or four deaneries.

I shared this thought the next day with a group of Christians I prayed with each week. They confirmed its rightness. The next day was full of meetings and so it was not until the following morning that I sat down after breakfast to put the idea in a letter to John Perry. As I was writing, Letty brought the day's mail into my study. Among the letters was one from John

Perry asking if we would be interested in a team coming up to the Cotswolds from Lee Abbey for a Mission in March 1983! This confirmed to us that the idea was of God. And so came about "The Celebration of Faith in the Cotswolds" involving four neighbouring Rural Deaneries and, in addition, two events in Gloucester Cathedral.

The 35 members of the Lee Abbey team were accommodated by different families, mainly in Chedworth. After an early breakfast they met at Chedworth vicarage for prayer and briefing. Then they scattered in small teams across the area to the various activities and meetings. Each secondary school welcomed a strong team for two hours on different days. There were coffee mornings, lunch meetings, seminars, meetings of young mothers and of retired people, and every evening a big meeting or service with imaginative music and sketches in one of the towns in the area. The 10 days concluded with a triumphant service on the Sunday night, in the large and beautiful Parish Church of Cirencester, which was packed to capacity.

Among the many who were blessed by this Celebration of Faith was a young couple who had come to live in the area very recently. They came to one of the evening services early in the Mission. She was keen, he was sceptical although he was sufficiently intrigued to come to an evening for men at the Royal Agricultural College a day or two later. On the Saturday they brought their two children to the Family, Faith and Fun Day and thoroughly enjoyed that. After the final service at Cirencester, they joined the queue coming forward for prayer and ministry. She re-committed her life to the Lord and he committed his for the first time. They then re-committed their marriage to the Lord. Since then they have moved on into lay leadership.

The three seminars on Christian Healing, led by a few of the Lee Abbey team during the Mission, gave valuable teaching on the subject and an impetus to the Ministry of Healing in the area. It began to be a normal and natural part of our overall ministry. For instance, at one of our Deanery Standing Committee meetings sometime afterwards, a farmer was late arriving. We knew he had not been well and had been to hospital for tests. We had just finished our coffee and were about to start the meeting when he came in. Our hostess quickly got him a cup of coffee and we waited for him to drink it and then began as usual with a relaxed time of prayer.

Our hostess noticed that our late arriver had difficulty in lifting the cup with both hands to his lips when drinking his coffee and so prayed for his health. As she did so I had the thought that we ought to offer him laying on of hands, so when our prayers were tailing off, I asked him:

"Would you like the laying on of hands for healing?" He readily agreed. The other four of us gathered round and took our time praying for him as we laid hands on him. Then we continued with the meeting, ending with another time of open prayer. The farmer prayed and thanked God for his healing, saying that at the beginning of the meeting he had not been able to to write, whereas at the end he was writing properly. Apparently he had been losing the use of his right arm and having uncontrollable twitches down the right side of his face.

As a result of the brain scan showing the probability of a tumour, an appointment was made with a neurologist in Oxford in expectation of surgery. When the farmer and his wife saw this surgeon, he was very quiet for a while and they wondered if he was praying as they were. They believed healing was already taking place and surgery was unnecessary. Eventually the consultant said: "There is definitely a slow growing tumour on the outside of the brain." To their delight, he went on to say that he was not going to operate as it might do more harm than good, but he would prescribe pills which would mean that it would be legal for him to drive. Our friend returned to his farm confident that the Lord was healing him.

When we had been praying and laying hands on him in that meeting, one of the committee who knew about it, prayed also for the healing of a long standing back problem. The pain completely went and has not returned.

Two years later, the farmer asked for another brain scan. It was completely clear with no mark of abnormality of any sort. He and his wife now help occasionally at the Harnhill Centre. I saw him recently looking extremely fit.

It would be good if everyone's need could be prayed for in the normal life and fellowship of the Church, but unfortunately that does not always happen and so there does seem to be a need for a more definite thrust of teaching and practice in this area of the Church's ministry. This is beginning to happen.

Through these years in the Cotswolds, we were discovering how rich and beneficial for the individual and for the community the Christian life can be when the vicar and people pray and work together with an expectancy that God loves to bless and to work miracles.

CHAPTER 10

THE MINISTRY OF CHRISTIAN HEALING

Most churches pray for the sick. The various parishes in which I served were no exception. We prayed for the sick in the services, the prayer groups and in our personal prayers. I became rather uneasy about the prayers in some prayer groups. They could degenerate into a mere recital of names, or on the other hand, the person praying was so concerned to tell God all the gory details that they seemed more interested in the sickness than in the healing. Moreover, most prayers in books, as well as extemporary ones, were for the sick, rather than the healing of sickness. When healing was prayed for, it often ended with the phrase: "if it be Thy will" in a tone of voice that implied that it might very well not be God's will. I became convinced that it is God's will that we should be whole.

Although God might permit illness and indeed use it to teach us something, yet He did not deliberately send it. He wants us to be healthy. So I began to pray for the healing of the sick according to His will, that is, in the way that He knows is best for us. To pray for the sick can be negative if one pictures the sick person continuing to lie in his sickness. Praying for the healing of the sick is positive if one pictures the person surrounded by the love and healing power of God. It is important to focus on the greatness, goodness and healing love of God, rather than on the sickness.

I knew, from personal experience, as many do, that God the Father is active today to bring good out of bad. I know Jesus as a living Lord and not a dead prophet. I know the Holy Spirit can direct and empower us in everyday affairs. These are the realities that should find expression in our prayers.

As my attitude to sickness and healing became more positive and my scepticism receded as I saw people healed, the subject took more prominence in my preaching. During the later years at Chedworth, when the Gospel for the day was the story of one of our Lord's healing miracles, I would suggest that the frequent incidents of healing in the ministry of Jesus pointed to the fact that God wanted to continue to heal the sick today, whether through doctors or the Church's prayers or a combination of both. God's desire was for us to be whole in body, soul and spirit; understanding the soul to consist of mind, emotions and will. These parts of our make-up are interdependent and affect each other because we are one person.

If the body is healed and other parts are left sick, more trouble will follow. Our need of forgiveness and to forgive others, our attitude of mind, our emotional hurts can all affect our physical health. And of paramount importance is our relationship with Jesus, through whom alone we are reconciled to God. Only as Christ becomes the centre of our life, can we come to wholeness and fullness of life.

As Jesus says: "I have come in order that you might have life - life in all its fullness." (John 10.10 G.N.B.)

"There is salvation in no one else" declares St. Peter (Acts 4.12).

In the beginning God created the world perfect:

"Behold, it was very good." (Genesis 1.31). Through man's original disobedience, sin, sickness, disruption and disharmony of every kind entered in and spoiled this perfect world. At the beginning God had given mankind "dominion over the fish of the sea, and over the birds of the air, and over the cattle and over all the Earth" (Genesis 1.26). Through his continuing sin, man allowed Satan to usurp more and more of that dominion until, when Jesus came, He called Satan, "the ruler of this world." (John 12.31) This "dis-ease", this rule of Satan, progressed through the centuries before Christ, and any efforts by man to reverse the process were quite inadequate.

God mounted his great rescue operation by sending His only Son to be the second Adam:

"As in Adam all die, so also in Christ shall all be made alive." (1 Corinthians 15.22). Only by Jesus coming and living, as man, a life of perfect obedience and taking upon himself all men's sins and their consequences on the Cross, and rising victorious over them, could men be freed from the grip of Satan and reconciled to God.

Jesus reversed the process begun by the first Adam and through His victory over Satan began the restoration of harmony, perfection and wholeness to man and the world.

"God was in Christ reconciling* the world to himself." (2 Corinthians 5.19) (* "restoring" - Living Bible).

"Through the Son, then, God decided to bring the whole universe back to Himself. God made peace through his Son's death on the Cross and so brought back to Himself all things, both on Earth and in Heaven." (Colossians 1.20 G.N.B.) Healing, as well as forgiveness, is a part of Christ's reconciling/restoring work. "He took our infirmities and bore our diseases." (Matthew 8.17). Healing and forgiveness are both available through Jesus. As a church we regularly ministered Christ's forgiveness to the penitent. Should we not also be ministering Christ's healing to the sick? Jesus told his disciples to go out to preach and to heal. We did plenty of preaching; what about healing? We seemed to leave that to the doctors, apart from our occasional prayers. The New Testament indicates that the Church has a fuller role, in co-operation with the medical profession, in the process of healing as part of Christ's restorative work.

The Acts of the Apostles is a book I have always found exciting and challenging. Before the Ascension, Jesus commissions his disciples to be his witnesses to the ends of the Earth, but first they are to wait for the power of the Holy Spirit. That comes upon them in Chapter 2. Peter immediately preaches to such effect that three thousand are converted and baptised, and then devote themselves to the apostles' teaching and fellowship, to the breaking of bread and the prayers.

In the next chapter Peter and John are going into the temple to pray by the gate called Beautiful, and there is a man, lame from birth, begging. Peter tells the man to look at them, which he does, expectant of a good donation. But Peter says:

"I have no silver or gold, but I give you what I have: in the name of Jesus Christ of Nazareth, walk!" (Acts 3.6) Peter helped the man to his feet and he accompanied them into the temple, leaping and praising God.

I had always had an uneasy feeling that the Church should be doing similar things today, and I was part of that Church, which was not. As the people in the temple flocked round them, Peter made it clear that he and John did not have the power to heal:

"Why do you stare at us as though, by our own power or piety, we have made him walk?" (Acts 3.12) This too spoke to me, for I knew that in my own power I could do nothing of spiritual worth. The first half of Chapter 15 of St. John, about the vine, had long been a favourite passage of mine, not least verse 5: "apart from me you can do nothing." I knew that

Christ's mission in the world could only be continued through the power of the Holy Spirit.

Since that experience in the little R.A.F. chapel, I knew something of the Holy Spirit's power, but often felt I needed more. I had experienced at times some of the gifts of the Spirit, but there was one gift which had been a mystery to me and about which I began to hear and read more often: the gift of tongues. At Oxford, in my large theological books, this had been explained as a phenomenon called "glossolalia". The scholars' explanation did not seem wholly convincing or satisfactory, but was the only one I knew.

About this time, a few parishioners in Chedworth were having some contact with what has been called charismatic renewal, either locally or further afield. One of them had a slight connection with Jackie Pullinger, who was soon to return to England for the first time, after her incredible experiences in the Walled City of Hong Kong, described in her exciting book "Chasing the Dragon", though that had not yet been published then. The parishioner asked if I would like Jackie to come and speak if she could fit it in. I readily agreed. And so, one memorable cold March evening, with every corner of Chedworth Church packed, she spoke for one and a half hours, and you could have heard a pin drop. Many stayed for ministry after her address. Later that night a few of us were clearing up the church and her hostess prepared to take Jackie back for a short sleep before an early start to her next engagement. I said a fond farewell to Jackie. In one sense I was looking at an ordinary English woman such as one sees in the street every day. But there was a difference. As she said goodbye, the love of Jesus just poured out of her in a way I have not seen in anyone else. I began to understand how God had been able to use her for such amazing miracles in the Walled City.

Earlier that day she had spoken in a village hall a few miles away. I had gone over to hear her. Afterwards I was privileged to join her for lunch in a nearby cottage with a few others. Lunch finished, I had the opportunity of a session with Jackie in an adjoining room. A month or so earlier I had made an abortive attempt to speak in tongues. Jackie now offered to pray with me again for this gift. Although she prayed and encouraged me for some while, I could manage nothing more that a grunt and a groan. Triad gangsters and drug addicts were a pushover compared with a sceptical Cotswold vicar.

Ten days later I was on my way to visit two parishioners in

Cheltenham hospital. As usual on such trips, while I drove along, I prayed for the people I was going to see, then moved on to sing aloud some hymns and praise songs. I stopped doing this and said to myself:

"I will have another go at this tongues business". I opened my mouth and out it poured and kept pouring. It sounded something like an Arabic language. Now I use this gift in my personal prayers, especially when unsure how to pray for a situation:

"The Spirit helps us in our weakness; for we do not know how to pray as we ought, but the Spirit himself intercedes for us with sighs too deep for words." (Romans 8.26) I often find myself speaking in tongues when driving to see someone recently bereaved or in deep trouble; the conscious mind is still able to focus on driving. Sometimes I use it quietly when laying hands on the sick. Singing in tongues is also a wonderful way of praising God with others.

Some of the laity in my parishes were gradually becoming involved in the ministry of healing. Initially I would ask a few people to pray in faith for the healing of a very sick person that I was about to visit at home or in hospital, at the time I would be there. Then, sometimes, I would take one or two with me to visit and pray for a sick person. I had done so occasionally over many years when taking communion to the sick in their homes. Then came the day when two friends of a woman in her 60's, who had just suffered a brain haemorrhage, came with me to the hospital to share in the ministry to her. The ward sister put the screens round the bed and the three of us prayed with the laying on of hands, upon the patient as she lay paralysed in bed. She was not expected to walk again, but within a few days she was doing so and was soon out of hospital.

Those of us who were interested in, and to some extent, involved in, the ministry of healing, felt that the time had come to introduce this ministry of the laying on of hands into our Sunday worship. A book that had recently been published and was on our bookshelf proved helpful. It was "Christian Healing Rediscovered" by Roy Lawrence. We discussed the matter in one of our quarterly joint parishes Worship Committee. Ideally I would like to have included the laying on of hands in the parish Eucharist but the extra time involved rules this out. In our multi-parish set-up I spent Sunday mornings chasing from one village to the next, to fit in services in as many churches as possible. My parishioners called it the Monte Carlo ministry. We settled for one Evensong a month in the main church at Chedworth.

To begin with, I often invited a visiting preacher, who had greater experience than myself in the ministry of healing, to speak and share in the laying on of hands. A few of our prayer group would arrive early in church to pray. After a short Evensong and sermon, the preacher, with one of our laity and myself with another, would go to either end of the altar rail, pray for each other and then invite anyone who would like to have prayer for a particular need, to come forward as there was a place available. Soon we had to have a further pair ministering in a side aisle. The service finished with a prayer of thanksgiving, a hymn and a blessing.

Some people we did not normally see in church began to attend, as well as folk from other parishes. With increased numbers, the service became too long for our regular Evensong worshippers. For this reason and also to prevent those who came from elsewhere, missing Sunday worship in their own churches, we moved the service to a Wednesday evening at 7.30 p.m. This was all right in summer, but not so good in winter; so we decided to hold the service at 3 p.m. on Sunday afternoons. This change also gave more leisure in the ministry and time for a cup of tea or coffee and a look at the bookstall after the service. This time after the service was especially useful for getting to know those from a distance and ensuring some follow-up.

Many people were blessed in these services in a quiet, undramatic way, though nonetheless miraculous for that. Some felt heat or tingling at the time of ministry. Others did not. Some received the help they sought, others something different. Few, if any, did not receive some blessing from the Lord. One local businessman had a recurrence of cancer. He was persuaded by a colleague to come to a service. He came forward, repented and gave his life to the Lord and received laying on of hands with prayer from two laity. When he undressed that night, he noticed that the lump had gone. This was confirmed by the specialist a few days later and as he left the hospital in a daze of gratitude he found his way to a nearby church to give thanks to the Lord. He is still enjoying a full and active life.

A young mother of about 30 came from a nearby town one Wednesday night; I will call her Pauline. She came forward for prayer for an arthritic back caused by a bad car accident some ten years before. She had also had a drunken father, which had given her some traumatic childhood experiences. In talking to her about these over a cup of coffee after the service, she suddenly said: "It is not those which worry me, but as a child I did something so wicked that I can never be forgiven." I invited Pauline to the vestry to tell me about it. She did so, although she had never told anyone else. It was not really that wicked, but she had been carrying this guilt all those years. I explained to her that Jesus had taken everyone's sins, however wicked, on the cross; so that all who turned to Him in repentance might receive total forgiveness. Through His victory over sin and Satan, we could have a new start with a clean slate.

Pauline had said sorry to God often enough in the past, but this time she was to do what she had not done before: accept and receive the forgiveness of Jesus as if she was receiving a lovely present from her husband. I pointed out that if she did not receive forgiveness, she would be spurning the cross and Jesus might just as well not have died as far as she was concerned. Pauline got the point, repented again of the sin and, as I pronounced the absolution, imagined she was receiving that gift of total forgiveness from the hands of Jesus. I then gave her laying on of hands and prayed for the healing of her back. She stood up and said: "I feel better already. It is as though I've had a tight spring coiled up inside me and it's suddenly been released. I feel so free."

I told her if she ever thought of her sin again, to say immediately: "Thank you God for forgiving me." I had three more counselling sessions with her over the next two or three months for inner healing of various hurtful childhood memories, to free her from nightmares and fears. She went back to work. A year or so later, after Harnhill was open, I saw Pauline there one morning digging in the garden as a thanksgiving contribution. I asked her about her back, amazed at the vigour of her gardening.

"Oh, I never think about it now," she replied.

"Isn't God marvellous?" I said as I thanked Him in my heart for Pauline's healing.

The news of our Christian healing services at Chedworth spread. Apart from people coming to us from a wide area, I began to get invitations to go and speak about Christian healing, run seminars, or help a church start a healing service. These invitations came from other denominations as well as from Anglican churches. Nearly always I would take a carload or a minibus load of parishioners with me. They would give a testimony where appropriate, assist in the ministry of laying on of hands and provide prayer backing. We also took our mobile bookstall with us wherever it was needed. These trips greatly helped the laity to mature and develop in their own Christian life and ministry.

The prayer basis and back-up was of paramount importance in the ministry of Christian healing in the parish. Like other parishes we had prayer groups and house groups for Bible study and teaching. I was constantly amazed that a person would grasp some Christian truth in these house groups which they had failed to understand from frequent sermons in church. There is always a danger that such groups can be looked on as "cliquey," so we made sure that an invitation to them was given in the Parish Newsletter and church notices. When I started a new one in the church in the early morning, I again made it clear that anyone from the five parishes was most welcome always.

I have always greatly valued the early morning quiet time throughout my Christian life. Mark 1.35 always struck me as important: "And in the morning, a great while before day, He rose and went out to a lonely place and there prayed". Jesus needed such an early morning time as well as other long periods of prayer. How could I presume to need less? My daily practice was to have my own quiet time at 6 a.m. or earlier. Then I went across to the church to ring the bell at 7.15 a.m. and say Morning Prayer with further intercessions. Meanwhile Letty was having her own quiet time at home. We had breakfast about 7.45 a.m. over which we shared our thoughts from our quiet time and checked our plans for the day, hoping to finish with a prayer together before the phone started ringing. I enjoyed the short walk to and from the church, especially on a fine morning; I would use the time to continue my prayers. As I left the church and closed the door to walk down the path, I would say something like: "I'm walking into the day with you, Jesus". One morning Jesus gave me a sharp jolt by replying: "Yes, with me, not two paces ahead!"-a necessary check to one of my many faults.

I so valued my early morning time with the Lord that I was always eager for others to take up the practice. As one way to encourage others, I invited and urged any parishioner who could, to come to church for an hour on a Monday morning at 7 a.m. or at 9.15. Three or four men normally came at 7 a.m. before they went off to work. Very often there were ten or more women at 9.15 who came after they had got their husbands off to work and children off to school. At that time many people were using the "Every Day with Jesus" notes by Selwyn Hughes for their daily Bible readings. At both times we went through the Bible readings and commentary for the day together. Then we shared any particular points that struck us before moving on to open prayer for the needs of the parishes and wider national and international concerns.

Quite often someone would have a particular problem for which they wanted prayer. One morning one of the men was dreading going to work because on that day he was to tell a colleague that the firm no longer required him. We prayed about it and asked the Holy Spirit to go ahead and prepare the way. He rang that evening to say how remarkably smoothly everything had been, with no animosity.

At 9.15 a.m. one Christmas Eve one of the women asked for special prayer for a baby grand-daughter who was critically ill and in intensive care. We felt it right to gather round her and pray for the baby's healing. She took a turn for the better that day and was out of hospital two or three days later.

A week later, at 9.15 a.m. on New Year's Eve, there was another urgent request for prayer. A young woman, who had lived in the village and was now married and living near Bristol, had rung me up the night before in considerable agitation. Her husband was in intensive care and the specialist had told her that there was nothing more they could do for him; he had had two operations already. The little group gathered round me and we prayed together for his healing. He held his own that day. The next day I felt compelled to re-arrange my programme, asked some of the parishioners to pray later that morning and drove down to the hospital. Although I had not told the wife I was going, as I parked my car, there she was getting out of hers two spaces up. We walked into the hospital together and immediately met the ward sister, who took us to the patient and put the screens round us so that we could pray with him without distraction. We prayed for his healing, gently laying our hands upon him. Within a few days he was out of hospital and has had no more trouble. He is in robust health to this day. I should warn that such rapid results did not always follow the laying on of hands with prayer, as I shall mention later, but when it does one is very conscious of the sovereign power of God at work. A praying group supporting the ministry is of great importance.

Sometimes when in the parish we got unexpected calls out of the blue. One night, I had just got into bed at 11 p.m. when the phone rang. It was from Bristol; a girl student I didn't know had been given my name. Sally was desperate, almost hysterical on the phone: could she come and see me straight away? This was quite unrealistic as she had no car or transport. I suggested she ring the Samaritans; she had already done that and was still desperate. What about the local church? Yes, she had had a helpful talk with the deaconess, but was still desperate. Sally was phoning from a call box so I took her number and rang back. I heard all her problems, talked with her for a long time and arranged to see her the next evening when unexpectedly I was free, a meeting having been cancelled. I then prayed with her for a long time on the phone and assured her that God would help her through the night. It was midnight when I replaced the phone.

At 6 a.m. the next morning, just as I was starting my quiet time, the phone rang. It was Sally; could she come straight away? No, I had a day full of meetings and engagements which I could not cancel, but I would meet her in Cheltenham at 6.30 p.m. as arranged.We prayed again on the phone, asking God to help and protect her through the day. That evening I picked her up and brought her back to the vicarage where Letty plied her with sandwiches and several cups of coffee. I had arranged for a woman in the parish, good at counselling, to come and share the ministry with me. She duly turned up after feeding her husband and we spent two and a half hours with Sally, bringing to the Lord for his healing, her problems and hurts and childhood memories and connections. Letty made up a bed and Sally slept soundly that night, which she had not done for a long time.

As I drove her to Cheltenham station early next morning, Sally told me how very much better she felt, so much so that she did not need to keep her appointment with the psychiatrist in Bristol that day. She was due to go into a psychiatric hospital the following Monday for a fortnight. I told her she must go and see the psychiatrist; she had nothing to fear. If she was better, the psychiatrist would confirm it and she would not have to go into the hospital. Sally rang me that evening and said this had proved to be so.

As Sally was speaking, I had a thought and said over the phone: "You are not expected at college next week, why don't you come down to Lee Abbey with our party from Monday to Friday?" Although we had such a large party that accommodation was stretched, I felt sure we could re-arrange the room bookings to fit her in. This we did and she shared a room with the parishioner who had counselled her with me. Those four days were vital for further counselling and healing. Sally finished her college course and got a job at the end of it.

I was due to retire from the parishes at the end of 1985 aged 65. Letty and I had set a few days aside in November to do some necessary jobs towards our moving. A few parishioners had gone to the Signs and Wonders conferences led by John Wimber and his team, some to London and some to Brighton. They came back so enthusiastic that they strongly urged us to go to another such conference in Sheffield. They had provisionally booked us in and would pay for us. Others were going to this conference from the parish and deanery. The dates exactly coincided with those I had set aside and, since they were so keen for us to go, we went. We did not regret it: the organisation was so efficient, the teaching so good and the ministry in the Spirit so effective.

The teaching clarified and confirmed a number of points for me. For instance, it confirmed a feeling which had been growing stronger in me for some years, namely that the Western philosophy of materialism and scepticism was one of the most undermining factors in Christian faith and action, including opposition to Christian healing.

Another thing that I had felt, but not formulated in my mind, was articulated for me by John Wimber, namely, that the gifts of the Spirit (apart from tongues) were not given us as a permanent possession: we do not carry them around with us in our pockets to be produced at will. Rather, if we are open to His Holy Spirit, God gives one or other of these gifts as it is needed, for the benefit of someone else in need, or for the benefit of the church at that time. This agreed with my experience.

I was also struck by the constructive and prayerful way John Wimber ministered to people's needs in the power of the Holy Spirit. There was no whipping up of emotions. The uplifting praise came before an hour of teaching. Then there would be a break and after we had re-assembled, John Wimber on the stage would quietly invite the Holy Spirit to come and minister to the people and then wait in silence. After a while the Holy Spirit, like a wave or gentle breeze, would move across the 3,000 or so people, ministering here and there according to needs; healing some, filling others with His love, releasing others. As the Spirit began to move on someone, members of John Wimber's team would quietly go and pray with him or her.

After one or two sessions, John Wimber encouraged members of the conference to pray with those near them. This had an interesting outcome: a person near us was seeking the gift of tongues and Letty and I moved over to pray with her. Letty had not received this gift herself, saying she already spoke too much in English without having a further language. But as she began to pray with this person for the gift, she found herself speaking in tongues!

The Wimber Conference proved a wonderful help and encouragement for a new venture which was about to begin.

CHAPTER 11

HARNHILL CENTRE

On December 16th 1984, Letty and I went for Sunday lunch to Harnhill Manor, 2 miles the other side of Cirencester from us. Although we had known Robert and Mary Henly for several years, we had never managed to visit their home. This time Robert had booked us up weeks ahead and then invited two other couples as well.

Harnhill Manor is a gracious house, set in beautiful but not too extensive grounds. It has a Georgian facade built onto a 16th century manor house. Robert had lived there all his life and Mary joined him when they married. They farmed the surrounding land very efficiently and created a friendly and welcoming atmosphere in the house. We enjoyed an excellent lunch. During coffee in the sitting room afterwards, I noticed on a side table the proof of a brochure for the sale of Harnhill Manor. I asked Robert:

"Are you thinking of selling?"

"Yes," he replied, "when we can find something suitable to move into. This is too large for us now and none of the family want to take it on." I did not think any more about it and soon had to leave for my next service. The following morning I wrote a thank-you note on the inside of a Christmas Card. As I was writing it, a strange and quite new thought entered my mind, like a gentle whisper. I added as a P.S. at the bottom: "What a wonderful

Centre of Christian Healing your lovely home would make!"

I forgot about it but three days later at about 9 a.m. Robert telephoned. He had just received my card and sounded very excited. He said: "I had a similar thought two years ago about the Manor becoming a Christian Centre." He had mentioned the idea to the Bishop and to another Christian leader, whom we both respected, but they had been careful to point out all the difficulties. Robert was now keen to go into the matter further. I suggested that we leave it there for the present, think and pray about it further and then share the idea in January at a meeting of some of our fellow Christians in the area. The meeting was a sort of follow-up committee of the Cotswold Celebration of Faith. Robert was on it, and I was chairman. In truth, I was apprehensive about the idea of a Centre, knowing that if such a project went ahead, it would mean a great deal of hard work, prayer and many miracles. I had only recently decided to retire in a year. Letty and I were looking forward to seeing a bit more of one another, for I had often neglected her, caught up in many responsibilities. We planned to travel a great deal and I hoped for some more fishing.

The January meeting took place in a farmhouse in the Chedworth group of parishes. After the other business had been dealt with, Robert and I shared the idea: a Centre where people could come for prayer, for healing, for counselling and for training courses; and from where small teams could go out to help and encourage churches to develop their own ministry of healing. I suggested that we did not discuss it then, but should go home and pray about it, and meet in a month's time at Harnhill Manor when everyone would be able to see the house.

The February meeting started early with a Eucharist in the small Norman church about 100 yards from the Manor, celebrated by the local Rector. Then we had a cup of coffee, a quick look round the house and settled in the sitting room: about sixteen of us. I spoke a little more fully about the concept and then suggested we were all quiet for 15 minutes, waiting on the Lord and inviting the Holy Spirit to reveal His thoughts and wishes to us. At the end of our period of quiet, I invited each to share in turn any thought, word, picture, prophecy or scripture that had come into their minds. I requested that each be honest and not mind if what they had to say seemed contradictory to what someone else had said. With one picture this seemed to be so, but by the end it was seen to complement and balance others. The overall message was quite clearly that we should go ahead in faith. There were prophecies, pictures, words and scriptures, one of which was Haggai 2.9:

"The latter splendour of this house shall be greater than the former, says the Lord of hosts: and in this place I will give prosperity (well-being, wholeness)."

It was agreed unanimously to go ahead, and in future meetings we always sought to be unanimous in any important decisions. Having so decided, it was proposed and agreed to form a small feasibility sub-committee to go into practical details of costs and what alterations and building works would be needed. Heading up that sub-committee was Peter Ralston, Church Warden of Cirencester Parish Church and a local businessman, who had lived all his life in Cirencester apart from the time he was flying in the R.A.F. during the war. He was a very great help in those early months; he had an architect friend who gave advice from that angle, and many other useful contacts. The feasibility sub-committee were to report back in two months' time.

At that meeting on 23rd April, the report was thorough and very positive. We decided there and then to elect a Management Committee. It was mainly selected from those in the room together with one or two other Christians whom we knew well and who had particular expertise that would be helpful. The Management Committee met for the first time on 11 May 1985 with the purpose of forming a Trust and obtaining a Trust Deed with which to approach the Charity Commissioners for registration. Our goal was to obtain an official number from the Inland Revenue so that we could seek covenants; we needed to raise £300,000 for the purchase of the Manor and the necessary alterations. We planned to produce and distribute publicity and appeal material, obtain architectural drawings and seek planning permission for the alterations.

Fairly soon after this first Management Committee meeting a few of us arranged through Robert and Mary to meet their three daughters and their husbands, one of whom was unable to come. We wanted to ensure that they were all happy about what was planned for their family home. As they were Christians, they were delighted, especially when they had assured themselves that whatever went on at the Centre would be Christ-centred. Their positive feelings for the project were confirmed when they discovered that we conceived of Christian Healing as Wholeness of Body, Soul and Spirit, which included the restoration of relationships between God and man, man and man, man and his environment. It was good for us and especially for Robert and Mary to know that they were wholeheartedly behind us. In fact the eldest girl, Sue and her husband David, continued to run the farm for a couple of years and helped a great deal at the Centre in all sorts of ways.

In those early days we consulted a good many people including the Bishop of Gloucester who was very supportive and Bishop Morris Maddocks, the Archbishop's Adviser for Health and Healing, who was enthusiastically helpful.

A firm foundation of prayer was started straight away, even before the first Management Committee meeting. With permission of the local Rector, up to twenty of us met in the little church adjacent to the manor for an hour of prayer and quiet on Tuesdays and Thursdays at 7 a.m. Alternate Thursdays would be a Eucharist and the laity would take it in turn to lead on other mornings. In addition, a longer period of prayer and waiting on the Lord, with fasting for those who wished, was soon started on Friday lunchtimes. This suited several who came to Cirencester to shop on that day. It took place in the Vearncombes' home in the centre of the town. They had recently moved from a lovely large house in a village in the Northleach Deanery, where they had been active in the church. Now, as well as taking a full part in Cirencester Parish Church, they were delighted to participate in the new venture at Harnhill. It was interesting the way the Lord moved others, over these months, to Cirencester or nearby, as though He were mobilising His helpers for the Centre. For instance, Peggy Allan-Ward was soon to move from Chedworth to live opposite the Vearncombes. She was already heading up the garden helpers.

As well as the regular times of prayer, we had periodic days or half days of prayer as the need arose over some particular issue or crisis, even an occasional 24 hour vigil of prayer. I had already seen how valuable such extended periods of prayer could be in parochial ministry.

One of the people who came to live in Cirencester about this time was Catherine Pither. She answered an advertisement for a companion-help to live in and look after a 94 year old lady in Cirencester. Her only hesitation in coming was that she wanted to be sure that she would be able to spend her spare time in some useful Christian service. She was a nurse by training, had recently been on the staff of the Divine Healing Mission at the Old Rectory, Crowhurst and previously had spent two separate periods with the Lee Abbey community in Devon. Peter Ralston brought her over to see me and I was able to assure her that with her background, she was a God-send to us and any spare time from her post could be fully used at Harnhill. She had the aura of a religious about her and one could easily imagine her in a habit in a convent, providing she was allowed to keep her sense of humour. When she came, she immediately took to our periods of prayer like a duck to water and often led them. With her previous experience at Crowhurst and Lee Abbey she was an invaluable asset during those early formative months and we co-opted her on to the Management Committee and also on to two of the sub-committees. She seemed a likely recruit as one of the staff when we opened the Centre.

These months of the summer and autumn of 1985 were very busy, with a lot of hard work and prayer; at times exciting, but at others frustrating and very testing. The work of the Management Committee was divided up into sub-committees: Buildings, Finance, Publicity, Appeals and Housekeeping, which at this stage was mainly thinking ahead to what furnishing would be needed at the Centre. Catherine Pither headed up this one with Letty and others. Peter Ralston headed up Buildings and Nigel Harris, a retired accountant now in his 70's was persuaded to be our Treasurer. Jane Lait, a farmer's wife who had been a key person under God in the Northleach Mission, the Celebration of Faith and much else, headed up the Publicity sub-committee, but soon handed over to Biddy Hobbs, a very attractive and lively Christian. Biddy was also lay-chairman of the Fairford Deanery. Major Sandy Vearncombe headed up Appeals. Later other sub-committees were to be added: Gardens, Friends, Programme Planning, Bookstall, Pastoral and Worship.

A list of sub-committees sounds dull, but it was full of personal stories and miracles: Katherine Hellyer and the Bookstall sub-Committee for instance. She was one of the Cotswold hunting set. When her children were fully fledged, she moved to a smaller, but still spacious house in Chedworth; her husband had been killed in a flying accident some years before. A year or two after she had arrived, I was praying one summer for another car and driver to get three post-confirmation youngsters up to camp in the Western Highlands, 600 miles away. In prayer, Katherine's name came; I dismissed it with "she wouldn't do it". With a week to go, the prayer was more urgent: again her name came to me. I rang. She would be delighted to come and cancelled her holiday in Italy. The camp intrigued and delighted her and she came again and again. It was the beginning of a closer association with the Church and the Lord. Meanwhile, her younger daughter had been thoroughly converted in London. When Katherine gave her life to the Lord, she asked Him how He wanted her to serve Him. He said: "Start a bookstall." She replied:

"Don't be silly, Lord, I'm a very slow reader and hopeless with figures." But she obeyed and it became a great blessing to the parish, the deanery and then at Harnhill.

A year or two after starting the bookstall, Katherine went to a healing service to ask for healing for a critically ill relative, who was wonderfully restored. As she was leaving the service, she realised that a painful and swollen leg, which she had not bothered to mention, was also healed!

Although it seemed slow at the time to us because of our eagerness and impatience, many of the practical things concerning the proposed Centre went through remarkably quickly, like the Trust Deed, planning permission, even the Inland Revenue Number. The finances also seemed to flow in quite well initially, all of which were causes for thankfulness in our prayer times. We did not feel it right to beg everywhere, or to run large lotteries; rather we wanted to give people the opportunity of having a part, as God directed them, in this new venture. It was along these lines that we produced our literature and approached possible donors. Some could give money, some practical help, some would become Friends and agree to pray regularly. Others could give in kind, even if they could not give money: a picture, a vase or a piece of silver, which could be used at the Centre or sold in an Auction Sale, which a local estate agent offered to organise free of charge the following spring. It was held in the Barn, raised £13,000 and greatly intrigued the regular dealers and others who came.

On our literature we always used Bishop Maddock's definition of Christian Healing given in a T.V. interview: "Christian Healing is Jesus Christ meeting you at your point of need". This quotation under a picture of the front of Harnhill Manor became our logo. We did not go for anything very glossy. It did not seem a right use of money, nor - for the same reason - did we employ a professional fund raiser. Instead, members of the Management Committee, once the literature was printed, took it and sent it to all the people we could think of who might help. In addition, Biddy Hobbs covered the local press and radio. Sandy Vearncombe went to the Public Library and ploughed through the huge Register of Charitable Trusts and began writing to any he thought might be the slightest bit interested. We did consult one or two friends who were in the fund raising business, who told us that we were doing the right thing, but not to think in terms of raising our target of £300,000 for three years at the earliest, and more likely five. We had planned to open at the end of May 1986; we put the date back three months.

Initially the money seemed to be coming in well, but when we reviewed the situation in the late autumn, the Treasurer pointed out that the great majority of money received had come from ourselves. The bulk was still to be found. With one or two exceptions, there had been very little response from Charitable Trusts. Some of those who had met and considered our appeal, had replied and said that Harnhill did not come within their terms of reference. Others said that as a matter of policy they did not support building projects or new untried ventures.

Christmas drew near and time for Letty and me to move from the parishes into a little terraced house in Cirencester for our "retirement". One or two members of the Management Committee were losing some of their first enthusiasm and wondering whether we had heard God aright. During one of our periods of prayer, someone had the thought of a large rallying service in Cirencester Parish Church. The vicar, Canon John Lewis, was contacted and the last Saturday afternoon in January chosen and agreed. Meanwhile Letty and I got caught up in our last, busy parish Christmas, with five beautifully decorated churches and full attendances at the various services, as well as all the parties, carol singing and so on. Naturally everyone wanted us to their parties and we had to disappoint several.

We moved in snowy conditions on December 29th 1985 to our little house in Cirencester. We had a job fitting in even the small amount of furniture and belongings we had kept, and the builders, who should have finished weeks before, were still around. A day or two later, still in the snow, a garage sale was held at Chedworth vicarage of the various items we had not sold or disposed of, the proceeds going to Harnhill. A bonfire burned for two days consuming all sorts of rubbish including hundreds of sermons and lots of files. More was added to it after the sale and with a sad heart I saw 35 years of parochial ministry come to an end.

The Farewell Party was held in the new Chedworth Village Hall on Sunday evening, January 5th. It was a happy, though moving, occasion and Letty and I were presented with a cheque for £4,000, enough for us to exchange our old small car for a new one. I also sold my old minibus a few weeks later to Fairford Youth Club for money to go to Harnhill.

Two days after the party on January 7th, we flew on a very cheap package holiday to Tunisia for a fortnight. We were exhausted, but within two days of sunshine and rest we had recovered enough to want to do all the interesting excursions including a Sahara safari and a Bedouin feast. There were also many more Roman remains to look at than I had expected.

Back in Cirencester, within a day or two I had a difficult Management Committee meeting. Finance, or the lack of it, still weighed heavily. I deliberately let the one or two doubters have their say to get it off their chests. I was intending then to seek to re-instill faith, but there was no need. A farmer friend of Robert Henly, who had given his life to the Lord at Lee Abbey a year or two before, had recently come on to the Committee. Suddenly he spoke up with great conviction saying:

"Where is your faith? God has told us to create a Centre of Christian Healing here at Harnhill Manor. We must trust Him and do so. The money will come in time."

It made it much easier for me to prepare a sermon for the big service of Thanksgiving and Dedication in a few days' time in Cirencester Parish Church; thanksgiving for a vision of the Harnhill Centre and an act of dedication to see it fulfilled.

God provided us a lovely, crisp, sunny winter's afternoon for that ecumenical service. A great many people came, some from quite a distance and there was a wonderful atmosphere of expectation and worship. The praise singing was led by the Cheltenham Mission Singers and the organist, John Beck, was at his most triumphant. From the local press cutting I see that I said:

"Jesus is alive and heals today as surely as He did when He strode across the hills and plains of Palestine, and as surely as He did through his disciples in the Acts of the Apostles. God wants us to be quite clear that He is Almighty, All Powerful and All Loving. It is not surprising at a time when the modern style of living brings great tensions and sickness, putting increasing pressure on the medical profession, that God should choose to revive the ministry of healing in his church to complement and work with the medical services. Moreover, God would seem to be using some of the wonderful healings through His ministry to remind the church and the world that He is indeed Almighty, All Powerful and All Loving, and that nothing is impossible with Him."

The Act of Dedication towards the end of the service was: "To the fulfilment of the vision for the Harnhill Centre of Christian Healing and Counselling". It was through "Total submission to our Heavenly Father of body, soul and spirit; time, talents and possessions. Through Jesus, our Risen Lord and Saviour by the Power of the Holy Spirit, to the Glory of God, His Father and Our Father. Amen, so be it."

After the Service, while many mingled for a cup of tea and a chat, many others came forward to the altar rail and side chapels for the Laying on of Hands with prayer for some need, or in some cases, to re-commit their life to God.

The collection of £1,100 was in itself a wonderful response. Although it was only a drop in the bucket of what was still needed, the whole service was a great encouragement to go forward with renewed enthusiasm and trust.

CHAPTER 12

LABOURERS INTO HIS HARVEST

From the beginning of the concept, we had envisaged that the Centre would be run by a small residential staff with a large number of outside volunteers. There had already developed across the Cotswolds a fellowship of Christians who knew each other, could pray naturally with each other and were ready to help in practical ways with any Christian project without neglecting their home parishes. Many of these were glad to help voluntarily in various aspects of the Centre from the beginning, though we always encouraged them first to take an active part in their local churches. For example, Katherine Hellyer, who is on the Management Committee and runs the Centre's Bookstall, has become Churchwarden in the village to which she moved.

When we considered the resident staff we needed for the Centre, we were limited by the amount of accommodation that was available in the Manor. The house had to be completely rewired, a larger central heating boiler installed and fire doors provided as required by the Fire Officer. Otherwise we did not have to make any structural alterations downstairs to the two large reception rooms, the dining room and pantry, the large kitchen and larder and the farm office.

The first floor of the Manor however, had to be completely re-organised, to provide for a through corridor, four double guest rooms, two bedsitters for the staff and a rather awkward flat for the Warden and his wife. Then the necessary bathrooms and toilets had to be installed, together with washbasins in each bedroom. In addition there was a single room halfway up the gracious stairs for a guest speaker, doubling-up as a counselling room during the daytime.

The position of Warden/Chaplain was all important. It would be possible for an ordained man to combine these positions. On the other hand, it would be possible to have a lay Warden and an ordained Chaplain. It would then be preferable that one of them should be single because of the accommodation. It was hoped that the wife of a married Warden or Chaplain would wish to participate fully. We had been advised that we needed someone in the senior position who had had experience of living and working in a community or residential home. I think now that this was a red herring, as there would have been a tendency for such a person to make Harnhill a copy of his previous centre, rather than seek with the others the unique plan God had in mind for Harnhill.

We made enquiries, contacted and interviewed a number of candidates for this senior position. As our literature began to circulate widely, others across the country offered their services. Always there were snags, or they were not right for the job or else God did not give them or us the green light to go ahead. It was this senior position which most concerned the Management Committee and Trustees. We had in mind possibilities for other permanent staff, but we wanted to settle the Warden's position first so that he could be included and consulted in the other appointments. But that was not to be and the position remained unfilled in spite of all the prayers and searching.

Early in September 1985 Ruth Warrington came to stay with us at Chedworth vicarage for a week. Letty was Ruth's Godmother. We had met the family while we were in Atherstone. Geoff, Ruth's father, was then a Jehovah's Witness and teaching at a local school for handicapped children. God laid it on my heart to go every morning after my 7 o'clock morning prayer in Atherstone church and drive the five miles to the Warrington home and share a time of quiet prayer and Bible reading with Geoff. He nearly always had some negative comment to share with me about the Church of England. One morning he had a cutting from the newspaper about an Archdeacon who had run off with someone else's wife. Part of his attitude went back to his disillusionment with his adult confirmation in Somerset a few years earlier, when his vicar had lent him a book and then had him "done." In contrast the dedication and commitment of two visiting Jehovah's Witnesses had attracted him. My main thought was not to rise in defence to Geoff's negative comments about the Church of England, but to admit we're not perfect, and needed help and prayer. Rather, I kept focussing on Jesus as "The Way, The Truth, The Life". After three months Geoff one morning suddenly broke down, confessed and gave his life to Christ.

Agnes, Geoff's gracious wife, was then prepared and confirmed in the Church of England and the children were baptised and the family home became a much happier place. Susan, the eldest of the five girls, was married to a local man. A few months afterwards Geoff accepted a new teaching post in the South of England, and then, some years later, moved to one in Queensland, Australia, together with the two youngest daughters. Now at Chedworth, nearly twenty-five years later, the sweet little girl to whom I told bed-time stories turned up at our vicarage as an attractive young woman with five years' teaching experience in Australia behind her. But she was also a sick woman.

Two years previously Ruth felt God tell her to leave teaching and "go and work full-time for Him". However, as with Abraham, God did not tell her where she should go. She had done a number of jobs, first in Australia and then in Europe, without ever feeling that she had arrived where God wanted her to be. When she contacted us, she had been staying for a while with another God-parent in Warwickshire. She came to us for a week and stayed for a year. She had a bad back and neck. She had seen a number of doctors and osteopaths but was no better. She also had had bouts of nausea and had become very thin.

We told her about the project of the Healing Centre in which we were heavily involved. Her heart immediately warmed to the concept, and she began to wonder if this was the place and purpose to which God was leading her. When she saw Harnhill Manor, which was to be the Centre, the words of Psalm 37 came to her mind: "Delight in the Lord and he will fulfil the desires of your heart. Trust in the Lord and do good; so you will dwell in the land and enjoy security". Naturally we prayed for her healing. The nausea disappeared, a relief after three years; the back, though improved, continued to give trouble from time to time. She immediately began to get involved in things in the parishes and with the Harnhill planning.

As Chairman of the Management Committee, most of the correspondence and administration went through me. Ruth began to help with this and was soon handling a great deal of it. When our move to Cirencester on retirement drew near, the question arose about Ruth. Our little terraced house was not large and Letty had used all her imagination and home-making talent to create a very gracious little dwelling, but naturally we had not originally planned for Ruth. However, upstairs there was what had been a box-room which Letty had planned as a television room. Now the TV came downstairs to the living room and a put-you-up settee couch but not much else, just squeezed in to the little room upstairs. This became Ruth's room for nine months.

From this base in Watermoor Road the pace quickened in our efforts toward launching the Harnhill Centre. Ruth typed on her little portable typewriter, phoned, kept all the records and got help from an office equipment shop across the road; they often let us have paper cheaply and also photo-copying at cut-price. I can picture now, working parties round our long dining table, filling envelopes to meet a post dead-line. It was useful also to have the Chinese Fish and Chip Shop only two hundred yards away. I recall asking Ruth on one of those days about a certain reference.

"You will find it in Box 3 under my bed" she said. Three cardboard boxes under Ruth's bed were the filing system for the Centre during those hectic months. "With God all things are possible." (Matthew 19.20.)

There was indeed a lot of hard work, but also a sense at times that God had everything under control. I have always found it difficult to get the right balance between human effort on the one hand and on the other resting in the Lord and allowing God's grace and power to operate, as expressed in the song: "Do not strive." Certainly in my early days in the ministry, once I saw what God wanted me to do, I would strive to achieve it. I would remember how Bill and I had urged one another on across the desert when we were fit to drop, and I would say to myself: "If I could do it for self-preservation, I can do it for God's Kingdom." That is perhaps why I finished up my curacy with pneumonia and pleurisy.

One of the scriptures that came to the fore more than once in the run up to the opening of the Centre, was that passage in 2 Chronicles 20: "The battle is not yours but the Lord's . . . You will not have to fight in this battle; take your position, stand still, and see the victory of the Lord on your behalf." The writer goes on to tell how the singers were sent ahead of the army to praise the Lord. Praise came to have an ever greater part in our Harnhill worship and prayer times. It was also brought home forcibly to me during those months as I put on the armour of God each day, how frequently the word "stand" occurs in that passage of Ephesians 6. We kept standing on God's promise for Harnhill, and yet the money and the staff did not materialise. God kept us "standing" and tested our faith until the eleventh hour, almost until the last minute.

Through the early months of 1986 we continued to pray and work for the money and resident staff we urgently needed for the Centre. Ruth was one obvious possibility for staff with her varied talents of administration, teaching and music. She was also a good cook, like her mother, and had catered for large households in her wanderings. I wanted to keep the options open as to where she might slot in to the Harnhill Team until we had some of the other positions filled.

One morning, March 20th 1986, a few of us met for a Eucharistic service in Harnhill Church in which we prayed specifically for Ruth: for inner healing and for her back. Her parents in Australia were praying for her at the same time. It was another step in Ruth's healing although her back continued to give trouble at times. In the afternoon Ruth went for a walk in the fields around Harnhill and during the walk the Lord gave her a song, both the tune and words based on the Scriptures from the service. The lovely song had a catching chorus in which all could easily join, beginning: "Rooted in the love of God". It was the first of many songs the Lord was to give Ruth in the coming years to enhance our worship and ministry at Harnhill.

Catherine Pither was also a possibility with her previous experience at Crowhurst and Lee Abbey, as well as her various gifts including prayer and care. But the big question was still who was to be the Warden/Chaplain. However, in May one very encouraging event happened concerning Ian and Ann Campbell.

Ian Campbell was a chartered accountant with a firm in Gloucester. He had given notice that he wished to retire in June 1988 at the age of 57. However his firm decided to amalgamate with a national firm and he was given the option to retire in June 1986 with a pension, which he accepted. Ann had been the Secretary of the Northleach Deanery and had been persuaded to become the Minutes Secretary of the Harnhill Management Committee. She had also been coming across to our 7 a.m. prayer time, and was therefore up-to-date with all that was happening towards the proposed Centre. I had envisaged their having a part to play in the outer team when the Centre was opened, imagining Ian might wish to continue with part-time accountancy in a private capacity from his home in Andoversford near Cheltenham.

Ann invited Letty and me for lunch the following Sunday, May 18th, after a gathering at Harnhill. We were free and so gladly accepted. Over lunch they shared with us their great hope to be involved together in full-time Christian work on Ian's imminent retirement. I told them they could be a real answer to prayer if they ran the Harnhill Office between them, covering the responsibilities of administration, finance and secretarial work.

"But" I added, "there is one real snag: accommodation. Unless we get a bachelor Warden, there will be no suitable accommodation in the house. You would need to live nearby and come in daily." They replied that they had already decided to sell their present house and look for something smaller now that the boys were away from home. They would look for something in the Harnhill area. Provided they could get a good price for their house, they would need little or no salary thanks to his pension. After the meal we prayed together and asked that the Lord would make the way clear and deal with the necessary house exchange.

As Letty and I left for home, we were in very buoyant mood and thanked God for his provision as we drove along in the car. That evening Ian and Ann had a phone call which sold their house without its going on the market. Within a week the senior partner of a local Estate Agency had found them a house within a mile of Harnhill, with all the accommodation they needed including a wired-in dog-run for their two English setters.

Although I knew Ann had been a company secretary and Ian had been used to running an office, I could not have forseen how marvellous they were to be once the Centre got going. They organised and set up the office to run most efficiently with a minimum of equipment and most of that second-hand, like my old filing cabinet. But more than that, they both kept their cool so wonderfully amid the hubbub around them, with people like myself popping in to check on various things. In addition, the phone would be ringing with Ann at her desk answering it so patiently. Ian would have his head in his ledgers which were always right up to date, yet he was ever ready to answer the interrupting questions calmly and clearly. Moreover, like other members of staff, they took their share in looking after guests, leading services, ministry and counselling. For the Christmas house party, Ian suddenly wrote two seasonal sketches and has continued to put pen to paper in this way at appropriate times.

The Warden was also to have his desk in the office next to Ian's, dealing with his correspondence, planning the programme and preparing talks. All three were marvellous examples of Christians working in harmony together.

At that important lunch with Ian and Ann in May, I had suggested to them that theirs would be a 9 to 5 job. They have often reminded me of that since! They liked to get to the Centre in time for the early morning prayers at 7 a.m, which were after all the basis of our endeavours. They then worked through to the evening meal at 6 p.m. Quite often one or other would stay on to work late or look after guests while the other went home to feed the dogs and do some household chores. It soon became evident to them that they needed to live in. Within months of opening the Centre, they converted, at their own expense, an old wash-house at the back of the Manor into a nice home, and let their house. But I am jumping ahead.

Two important things happened at the beginning of June 1986. The builders moved in to carry out the necessary alterations. This was only with the approval and permission of Robert Henly, for we still had nowhere near enough money to purchase the building and exchange contracts. The other thing was that on the first Wednesday evening of the month, with the permission of the local Rector, we began weekly services of Christian Healing in the little church near Harnhill Manor. Some of us had been responding to invitations to go out to churches to speak about Christian Healing and about the proposed Centre. Moreover, requests were constantly coming in now for help for those in trouble.

Once the Centre was opened we also started a healing service in the setting of the Eucharist at 10.30 a.m. on Fridays in addition to the one on Wednesday evenings. These two services have continued through all weathers and through holiday periods. One Wednesday evening no-one from outside could get to the service because of deep snow, so those in the house had one among themselves, praying for each other. These healing services contain all the necessary ingredients of praise, scripture, teaching, penitence, prayer, laying on of hands for those who wish, and thanksgiving. Afterwards there is always an opportunity to meet informally over a cup of tea or coffee, and to look at the bookstall.

With the Trustees gladly accepting the offer of Ian and Ann to come and run the office, we were able to consider other appointments. Ruth opted for the responsibility of catering and cooking. She had already given the whole of her worldly wealth to Harnhill, namely her superannuation from five years' teaching in Australia. When the Centre opened, she would get accommodation, her keep and a small allowance. Catherine Pither would be the housekeeper on the same terms, looking after the rooms and organising the outside voluntary help that she needed to keep the place clean and tidy and the bedlinen laundered and ironed.

Still we needed a Warden/Chaplain and wife, and time had almost run out. We were to open the Centre in three months time and plans for it were well advanced. Three bishops were booked for the ceremony, among others. Invitations were being printed. Letty and I began to think that we would have to move in and fill the role ourselves to start with but we did not really believe this to be right at our ages. In any case, it was important for the Warden and his wife to be there at the start of the enterprise in order to forge together the resident team and develop a pattern of communal life for the future.

On June 24th 1986 I was attending the annual meeting of the Greater Chapter of Gloucester Cathedral. As usual we began in the morning with a Eucharist in the Lady Chapel. During the service I was praying again about the need for the right person for the post of Warden/Chaplain. I had hardly lifted the matter to the Lord when into my mind had come the name of Hugh Kent. I had known Hugh and his attractive wife, Hilary for twenty-five years. As a curate he had been in the Coventry Diocese and had played cricket for them when I was captain. He followed me to Gloucestershire and we continued to meet on the cricket field. In fact, it was Hugh who scored the winning run in our famous Church Times Cup final victory against the Liverpool Diocese. More recently I had handed over to him the job of secretary of the Diocesan Missionary Council. His name had first come into my mind months beforehand, but I had immediately dismissed it, mainly because I thought his children were younger than they were and we did not have the accommodation for a family. In any case, at that time we were looking for someone who had previous experience in living and working in a Christian Community.

When I got back from Gloucester Cathedral that evening, I immediately rang the Kents. Hugh was out and Hilary answered the phone. I said:

"I know it's a strange question to ask, but how old is your youngest?"

"Fifteen", came the reply, "but why do you ask?"

Ignoring that question for the moment, I asked another:

"Does he live at home or is he away at school and are the others fully fledged?"

"Peter is away at Monmouth and the other two are fledged. But why do you ask?"

I drew a deep breath praying at the same time.

"I don't know whether you have heard of the proposed new Centre of Christian Healing at Harnhill."

"Vaguely" she replied. I continued:

"I was wondering whether you and Hugh would be interested in becoming the first Warden and wife." Hilary's answer was strange, but can be accounted for by the fact, as she told me later, that her heart leapt within her. She said: "Oh, Arthur! What are you doing to us? !" I asked her to tell him to pray about it and ring me in the morning. Later that evening Hugh rang to ask more details and to say that initially they were interested, but would pray about it and phone again in the morning.

In the morning he confirmed their interest. They were thinking of moving anyway and the Bishop had already offered them another parish; they would naturally have to consult him fully, and go and see the new parish as a matter of courtesy. Recently however, they had felt themselves to be at a crossroads and did not feel sure that the Lord wanted them to go to another parish and just do what they had done before. We agreed on a date in the near future for them to come over and see Harnhill and meet the Trustees.

It was a lovely sunny afternoon for the visit of the Kents and, after looking round the place, we had tea on the lawn with the Trustees. Hugh and Hilary liked all they had heard and seen, even the rather poky Warden's accommodation still in the process of alteration. However, it would rather depend on what their youngest son, Peter, thought about it. He was home for half-term the following weekend. One possibility for him was to do up a small outhouse, Jack's office, which consisted of two very tiny rooms. They thought he might like that as a separate den of his own and be prepared to do it up himself, with father's help. If they came, Peter agreeing, Hugh would need to get the Bishop's approval and give three month's notice to their present parish. After they had left, the Trustees were able to express their thoughts. We had never had such unanimous approval of any of the other candidates, even of one or two excellent ones, who had, in the end, decided against coming.

Peter came and liked the idea of a den: "Fab!" was his comment. Hugh and Hilary went to see the other parish and did not feel it right anyway. The Bishop was most helpful and supportive and, in correspondence with me, asked that Hugh should be called Chaplain and Warden. As a Chaplain he would remain on the Diocesan Register, could serve on the Diocesan Synod and continue as secretary of the Diocesan

Missionary Council - and play in the cricket team! The Bishop would ask the Diocesan Board of Finance to continue paying his clergy insurance towards his pension: about £1,000 a year. The Centre, of course, would pay his salary, so, with less than two months to the opening, we had a Chaplain and Warden. Hugh had some leave due to him and would come and camp in the grounds over the period of the Opening in order to work on Peter's Den, on the decorating of their flat and to see the Centre started off, working out the daily routine together as a resident team. Then he and Hilary would have to return to St Aldate's, Gloucester for another month, taking up residence at Harnhill at the beginning of October.

God knows best. Had I known Hugh and Hilary far better than I did, I would still not have realised how good they would be as Warden and wife. Not only were they right for the job, the job was right for them: for the next stage of their ministry and for their own spiritual growth and development.

Hilary is a wonderful hostess, warm-hearted and welcoming: she quickly puts guests at their ease. People sense her care for them. She is also very compassionate and feels deeply for the fragile or those in trouble. If tears come easily to her, that is good; it releases others through the gift of tears. Her musical talents have also been a very great blessing.

Knowing Hugh on the cricket field and at committee meetings gave me little insight into his qualities of leadership. Again, he is able to put people at their ease and yet the Holy Spirit often gives him deep insight into their hidden needs. He is compassionate and kind and yet able to be firm when occasion demands, as it often does in leadership. One of the qualities I have valued is his ability when things go wrong, to say immediately aloud: "Praise the Lord." My normal reaction is to keep quiet but feel annoyed. I may then turn to the Lord in my mind after a moment or two. But Hugh's instant "Praise the Lord!" means that he and those near him immediately turn to God, which puts the awkward situation into its proper perspective, reminding us that God is in command.

They both enjoy fun, have a good sense of humour and are practical. Hugh, in our training courses, and at other times, is impatient with what he calls: "Yap". He wants to make the Gospel practical: to apply to real life whatever the subject is and not just to talk about it. Another great quality is his readiness to admit a mistake and apologise.

As I have watched them handle situations and guide the Centre in its growth, I have just marvelled that God knew long beforehand how right they were for the job. He knew what qualities were there long before we did. Maybe even Hugh and Hilary did not realise themselves that some of those qualities were in them. As in the desert when the rain comes, up shoots unexpected growth from unseen seeds. So with them, and all of us, when the dew of the Holy Spirit falls upon us, there can be an unexpected and wonderful harvest, so that the "Desert becomes like the Garden of the Lord." (Isaiah 51.3)

October 1986 saw the resident staff of Hugh and Hilary, Ian and Ann, Catherine and Ruth being welded together as a team for God's service at the Centre, and learning how to mobilise and use the voluntary help of the Outer Team. Before long, the harvest was beginning to grow and ripen.

CHAPTER 13

BIRTH OF THE CENTRE

With the appointment of the Chaplain/Warden the worst of the labour pains were over and the birth was imminent. But there were still some agonising moments, not least for Robert and Mary Henly We were still well short of our target of £300,000 and did not have nearly enough money to purchase the house as well as to pay the contractors. Robert came to the rescue by offering to give us a low interest mortgage to enable us to meet our obligations. Ian Campbell was now taking over the finances, or lack of them, from Nigel Harris. Ian and Robert worked out the details of this mortgage arrangement which the Trustees gladly accepted.

However, Robert's accountant and solicitor, who had served him faithfully and well over many years, had great difficulty in coming to terms with it all. The Robert they had known had been a very successful farmer and able financier, yet here he was being unbusinesslike and squandering his assets. Naturally they delayed, double checked and held things up as long as they could. They openly expressed their doubts and scepticism that we would ever raise the money or become a going concern. No doubt they thought Robert would soon come to his "worldly" senses. We kept praying for them and for Robert. He stuck to his convictions. With his permission the resident staff were to move in and the opening ceremony was to take place, although the property did not belong to us. It was several weeks later that the exchange of contracts finally took place. All sorts of contingency clauses were included in the contract, in case we did not come up with the money or the Centre proved a flop.

I said: "the resident staff were to move in," but it was not as simple as that. By the beginning of August the building work, central heating and rewiring were more or less finished. To save expense, we had decided to do the interior decorating ourselves with voluntary help. Peter, the Church Warden of Cirencester Parish Church, who had been such a help with all the practical and legal side of the venture, offered to head up the decorating team during August. He was able to obtain the materials from a Cirencester dealer at a reasonable rate. He persuaded the Vicar of Cirencester, Canon John Lewis, to ask for volunteers from the congregation. I happened to be in church that morning. At the end of the service, a Yorkshire lady who had recently moved to Cirencester, Diana, came up to me and offered to help: "I'm no good at painting, but I can scrub floors and wash down paintwork if that's any help." I linked her up to Peter's wife, Margaret, who was standing nearby. A few days later I went into Harnhill Manor and there was Diana making tea for all the helpers and looking radiantly happy. I remarked on her cheerfulness and she said: "Yes, I've never been happier in my life. And what's more, I have had insomnia for years. Now I'm sleeping like a log!"

Ian and Ann Campbell had moved out of their house, but were not able to get into their new one yet. Throughout August they slept on a mattress in one of the Manor bedrooms while they decorated the next, moving from room to room on their mattress and working all hours with great cheerfulness. I'm sure it was not how they had envisaged spending their first weeks of retirement!

Another couple Peter contacted from Cirencester Parish Church moved their motor-caravan into the grounds of the Manor as a base from which to work. The wife was a beautiful needlewoman and had volunteered to make all the curtains, which she did most perfectly. Meanwhile her husband turned out to be a skilled joiner by hobby and was able to perform all sorts of delicate woodwork jobs around the house. Sandy Vearncombe was another who helped in this way.

As we drew near to the opening the painting and decorating were falling behind schedule. A couple from my last parish of Chedworth, who had helped me with recent Youth Camps in Scotland, came to the rescue, together with a group of teenagers who had been on those camps. They slept in tents in the Manor field for the last weekend before the opening and worked from early morning until late at night, decorating the long downstairs passage, the two toilets and the dining-room. They had an hour's break on the Sunday morning for a Eucharist which I took for them and a few other helpers, mostly still in their dungarees. The youth got a good deal of paint on themselves and there was a great deal of laughter, but they cleaned up well when they had finished. The builders, who were still around, complimented them on their workmanship and asked if any of them wanted a job! Many people worked up to the last moment but, just in time, everything was ready for the opening.

August 30th 1986 was a lovely fine day. Bishop Morris Maddock and his wife Anne, who had greatly encouraged us in our endeavours to establish the Centre, stayed overnight in the Manor. In the morning we began in the Church with a service of dedication and commissioning of the inner and outer teams in the setting of Eucharist. After coffee, we accompanied the Bishop all round the rooms of the house and the outbuildings while he splashed them with holy water, cleansing and dedicating them in prayer to the Lord's service. After a buffet lunch, we got ready for the opening ceremony. After all the months of labour and prayer, we could hardly take in the fact that at last we had come to the point of birth.

Over two hundred people turned up for 3 p.m. and overflowed the barn in which the service was to be held. After opening prayer and praise, Bishop Cuthbert Bardsley, who had been very supportive of the venture, gave one of his typical clarion-call addresses, rallying the troops to go forward in faith. It was lovely to have him there in such good form. I had served under him for many years in the Coventry Diocese and had seen many people blessed when he led our Northleach Deanery Mission. Ruth sang her song. The Rev. Vernon Gotten, the leading Methodist minister in Gloucester, read a lesson; a small team of us had helped at his church some two years earlier when he started healing services there. Bishop John of Gloucester spoke encouragingly: he pointed out that we at the Centre were not setting ourselves up as experts and totally whole people. All of us were Walking Wounded on the road to wholeness, ministering to each other.

We all moved on to the terrace in front of the Manor where Bishop John led us in the formal act of dedication and blessing, and declared the Centre open. In a final symbolic moment Robert and Mary Henly planted two ornamental trees, one silver and one gold to commemorate the day, and as a reminder of the first healing miracle of the church, when Peter and John said to the crippled man at the entrance to the Temple:

"I have no silver or gold, but I give you what I have: in the name of Jesus Christ of Nazareth, walk." (Acts 3.6)

We walked to the other end of the lawn for a celebration tea. The Centre had been born and there was a sense of relief as well as rejoicing. When a child is born, the parents, family and friends are normally thrilled with the miracle of new life. In fact, that new life had begun many months beforehand at conception and had been growing ever since. So it was with the Centre. Though it was now born for all to see, the Centre's life had begun months beforehand in the fellowship and prayer of those committed to the concept. No doubt, in God's mind, it had begun æons before that. We were always conscious that it was God's idea and not ours. The lovely buildings and grounds of the Manor provided the new setting for this new life now manifest.

The development of a newborn child in the early months is often more noticeable to those outside the family than it is to those who are with the child day by day and hour by hour, to whom the child's growth seems gradual and natural, except for outstanding stages like the child's first word or step. It was a bit like that with the Centre. The resident team gradually gelled as they worked and prayed together, developing the routine of the house. The outside team of volunteers, who had been helping for months to enable the Centre to be born, now dovetailed into those routines. New facilities were being established by the two complementary staff teams as they were needed. The development of this new child was, on the whole, gradual and steady, without too many growing pains, thanks to the grace of the Holy Spirit.

Most of the voluntary outside helpers were friends from across the area who had been to our annual parties to Lee Abbey and had taken part in our Celebration of Faith in the Cotswolds in 1983. From time to time others were added and blessed by God.

Soon after we started the healing services in the little church in June 1986, a local businessman, Mike, came one Wednesday evening, encouraged to do so by his doctor. He was desperate. He woke each morning at 4 a.m. with black depression, had a drink problem, chain-smoked and was suicidal. I met him outside the church before the service, he was having a quick smoke and trying to pluck up the courage to go inside. I was able to put him more at ease by telling him about the gentle way the service was conducted. As he came forward at the appropriate time, for prayer and laying on of hands, Jane, one of the pair towards whom he was moving, had the word "anger" come into her mind. He did not look an angry person. On the contrary, he gave the appearance of being jovial and without care. But Jane was not diverted and gently led round to it and asked the Holy Spirit to come and reveal to Mike if there was anyone with whom he found it difficult to get on, now or in the past.

Immediately into Mike's mind came his mother, though he had not thought about his early bad relationship with her for years. He sought and received forgiveness and then the two ministering prayed for the healing of his other problems. The next day he did not wake until 7 a.m. and without depression. A week or two later he went down to put things right with his mother. Other things followed, like a total commitment of his life to Jesus, as Mike continued towards wholeness. His teenage son turned up to a Wednesday healing service some time afterwards, intrigued by the change in his father and he too gave his life to the Lord. Before very long, Mike and his lovely wife Mary were themselves ministering to others at the healing services.

One of Mike's talents was to play the guitar. He began to collect together a music group to lead worship at Harnhill and elsewhere. One of the group was a flautist, Carol. Many months earlier I had been to speak at one of the series of ecumenical Lent talks in a Methodist church in a town in the next county, Wiltshire. A week or two later, the Methodist minister rang up and asked if I would be prepared to see Carol. She and her husband came over one night to our little house in Cirencester. I was glad he was there with her, as I felt more inadequate than usual; Carol was in such deep depression that she found it almost impossible to communicate. She also went into a sort of tension fit, clenching her hands so tightly that her fingernails drew blood from her palms. At times she would writhe and moan on the floor. She had previously had a period of depression and recovered. This second one had been triggered off by a miscarriage, for she desperately wanted a child. Her husband was a great help; so patient and kind, although after some months it began to get him down. Carol not only came with him at appointed times, but, having her own car, was liable to turn up at any time. She was, of course, seeing her own doctor and attending a psychiatric clinic. She improved a little and certainly was soon able to communicate better, but there would also be set-backs and tension fits. Our Labrador dog was most sympathetic and played her part. Neither Carol nor her husband had liked dogs, but they became very fond of "Lucky"..

Early one evening Carol turned up unexpectedly in a very poor way and stayed on. In fact, she was in no fit state to drive home and didn't want to anyway. As on previous occasions, I rang her husband as soon as I knew he would be home from work, and told him where she was. I also said that, although there was no hurry, it might be as well if he were to come over later, as

I did not think she should drive. He said he would get himself something to eat and come on later. We had further talk and prayer when he came and at about 10.30 p.m. the Holy Spirit suddenly got through to Carol and gave her a picture of a church with a big, plain wooden cross on the altar, with her kneeling before it and committing her life to Jesus. The Harnhill Centre was a long way from being opened, nor had the healing services yet started in the church, but her picture was clearly that of Harnhill church and altar on which was just such a cross. I told her so and we agreed to go over to the church and make the picture a reality. She had perked up considerably and was able to drive, following me to the church with David following her. There, kneeling before the altar, at 11 p.m. she re-committed her life to the Lord and at her request said all the words of the hymn "Take my life and let it be consecrated Lord to thee".

Carol was not free from her depression for some months, but it was a turning point. Not long afterwards the healing services started and later the Centre was opened and Carol was able to continue to receive counselling and ministry from several of us. She became well enough to help at the Centre in various ways and to play her flute in Mike's musical group: "Vision". After about eighteen months, now well, she became pregnant and gave birth to a lovely girl, Alice. She now has a second child.

With the Chaplain/Warden and his wife duly installed in October 1986, the life of the Centre became vibrant and vigorous and at times hectic. As with a new-born child, a daily routine had to be worked out. The pattern of 7 a.m. prayer on Tuesdays and Thursdays continued and some of the outer team came to join in. The Friday lunchtime sessions continued for a while until the 10.30 a.m. healing service within a Eucharist was started. Then a period of Scriptural meditation and waiting on the Lord took place on Wednesday afternoons in preparation for the evening service. In addition, before each Wednesday and Friday healing service there would be half-an-hour of preparatory prayer and praise and seeking the Holy Spirit for words of knowledge or prophecy for the service. Those ministering the laying on of hands or participating in any way in the service, were expected to be there for that preparation time. It was a bit of a rush on a Wednesday evening for those who had been at work all day, to get home, eat, change and travel several miles to the Centre. But the Holy Spirit restores and refreshes so quickly.

On weekdays other than Tuesday and Thursday, the resident team met at 7.30 a.m. in the house for devotions and then, over breakfast, planned the day before taking up the breakfast trays to guests in their rooms. Each guest room has facilities for making hot drinks whenever required. Outside helpers came in about 9.30 a.m. and would be given their work by Catherine Pither in the house, and by Ruth Warrington in the kitchen. At 10.30 the gong would sound for morning prayers over a cup of tea or coffee. These were very informal but none-the-less helpful; guests and helpers joining in together. One of the house team would lead and often just read slowly the scriptures from: "Living Light" one by one, invite comment, pray and sometimes sing a hymn or praise song. On days when we had a course or training seminar, the guests and helpers would join in the opening worship at 10a.m. On Sundays, guests would normally be invited to go with the house staff to worship in one of the local churches, unless it was a special weekend, when an appropriate service would be held in Harnhill Church, which normally only had a parish service once a month. Each evening in the house would finish with a short act of worship, sometimes Compline, about 9 p.m. or a little after.

The guests who come to stay vary a great deal in age and in needs. Some come for two or three days' rest, refreshment and quiet. Some come to participate in a particular course. Some come with hurts, illnesses, depression or other specific needs. While seeking to be flexible, we made it a rule from the beginning that we would take no cases needing nursing and no-one for longer than a fortnight. We also sought to have not more than one depressive staying at a time, though that does not always work out. Those taking medication are asked to bring a note from their doctor. One of the Cirencester practices is always on call should we need a doctor in a hurry. When guests arrive, mainly on a Monday or Friday, the house team welcomes them and seeks to help them feel members of the family. They are encouraged to join in the daily worship and the healing services, but are never compelled to do so. Individual counselling is always available if needed, but it is not forced upon guests, who are also free to attend any course or training day which might be running during their stay. Some, including clergy, come for just a day visit or simply to "flop". The charges are extremely reasonable and there is a bursary fund to help those who cannot pay. No-one is ever refused through lack of money. People come through hearing about it on the grape-vine, picking up a brochure somewhere, or because their minister, doctor or social worker recommends it.

We also became more widely known through a few seconds on a television "Songs of Praise" programme transmitted from Cirencester Parish Church. One young woman who gave a testimony and chose a hymn, told the interviewer how she had been helped by people at Harnhill. Intrigued, the television crew came and took a few shots.

People come to Harnhill from near and far and through all sorts of contacts. One young mother and baby from a town on the South Coast came for a fortnight, sent by her social worker. We never did find out how the social worker knew about us. The young mother responded whole-heartedly to the welcome and love she received at Harnhill. She knew little about Jesus but lapped up everything she was told or read about Him. She gladly gave her life to Jesus in the second week. We had a marvellous first birthday party for her baby a day or two before she left. Another guest, who was staying at the time, had a married daughter who was a keen Christian and lived near the young mother. He contacted his daughter to ensure that there would be a continuation of Christian care and the opportunity to integrate into a Christian church. It is marvellous how God arranges these things!

Frequently guests write to express their gratitude: "Harnhill is a place of true peace and wholeness", wrote one. "I am so much better", was a frequent remark. "We experienced such a beautiful feeling of being wrapped in the peace and love of God!" said another.

As well as guests coming to stay, other people come for one or more sessions of counselling without being residents. Some of us have been counselling people in an unofficial way for years. Such counselling consisted mainly in listening, care and prayer. But before the Centre opened, a number of us had been to the preliminary and advanced counselling courses at The Old Rectory in Crowhurst, Sussex. We also had Mary Evans from there to stay for a few days and she ran a course in the unfinished house at Harnhill. We continue our training mainly through the excellent prayer counselling courses organised by "Wholeness Through Christ". Later we were to receive, with great gratitude, into our outer team Deaconess Dorothy Knowles. As well as having a long and fruitful pastoral ministry in parishes, she had helped to run "Wholeness Through Christ" courses. On retirement she had taken a year's course at Exeter University on counselling and then came to join us. What a blessing! She concentrated mainly on assisting the house team in the counselling of resident guests. She became a Deacon and Assistant Chaplain of the Centre to Hugh Kent, with whom she had previously worked in a parish in Coventry.

The organising of the non-residents who came to the Centre for a counselling session was undertaken by Mrs. Jane Lait, the lady with the broken neck I had ministered to in hospital years before. She had been on several counselling training courses. Some of the people who came for counselling had been to a healing service and it was suggested then that they needed a longer time than it was possible to give them during the service. Others would just ring up and ask for counselling, giving some of their needs. Jane coordinated those of us of the outer team who felt called to this ministry and had received some training.

She would match counsellers, times and those requesting help with skill and tact and with great efficiency. As with the ministry of the laying on of hands, the counselling was always done by two people. A man would always be counselled by one man and the other could be male or female. Similarly, the pair counselling a woman would always include a woman. The advantages of counselling in pairs and the dangers guarded against by this practice are manifold and are given in many of the books on Christian couselling. We always allowed one-and-a-half hours for a session and in some cases longer. Tea and coffee were available, a box of tissues and anointing oil always on hand. Sometimes a person would need several sessions, sometimes the matter could be dealt with in one, even though it had been anticipated that more than one would be necessary. This was so with two cases of anorexia.

One girl of fifteen, who had been under medical care for some while, and was surrounded by the prayers and care of her family and church, had nevertheless become a mere shadow of six stones and was given six months to live. She was completely healed in a two-hour counselling session at Harnhill, the Holy Spirit revealing to the counsellors the root of the problem. At the end, Jane, who normally takes her own lunch with her when she is doing two or three counselling sessions, asked the girl if she would like a sandwich. "Yes, please!" she said enthusiastically and proceeded to devour most of Jane's lunch. Her father wrote in his church magazine: "The privilege of being witness to a miracle will be with us for the rest of our lives".

The other girl was about a year older and had recently done

brilliantly in her "O'-levels at a Grammar School where I was a governor. Anorexia had quickly set in and she had just had a traumatic time in hospital and was worse. She came with her mother and we had a brief session together and then, as the Holy Spirit guided, a time with the girl on her own, which included prayer and the laying-on of hands. She improved rapidly and a month or two later was baptised in her Baptist church. She came to a healing service at Harnhill exactly a year later with her mother and father to give thanks. She did very well in her 'A'-levels and went on to college.

Some cases, of course, take longer, especially those who have been on strong doses of medication for some years. As they reduce their drugs, with their doctor's permission, they often need a lot of support and care to cope with the withdrawal effects. The weekly services of Christian healing were a help here, but the person would sometimes need on-going counselling as well. We are aware of the danger, however, of the person becoming too dependant on the counsellers rather than on God, and always encourage the strengthening of the person's relationship with Jesus and fellowship in their local church. We never charge for counselling, but the person can make a donation to the Centre, if they wish.

From the beginning we saw ourselves as a resource centre for churches of all denominations. We exist to help them in any way we can. Often we are invited to go and speak about Christian healing, run a seminar, or help with a healing service. It was a particular joy after going to churches of other denominations to be asked to take a healing service in a Roman Catholic church, with the lovely, elderly, humble priest himself coming forward for prayer and laying on of hands. A car load or two will go out from Harnhill for this purpose and occasionally two teams will go out to different places at the same time. On a few occasions we have been asked to lead a day of renewal for a church and twice for a diocese and were happy to do so. We were also invited to lead a day on the practical aspects of the ministry of Christian healing at Trinity College, Bristol. As a result, in subsequent summers, we have had the joy of having a student from there come for two or three months to live and work with us at Harnhill as part of their training. Once each month, a weekend is made available for churches to use the facilities of the Centre, to run a day or weekend conference themselves with or without our teaching help, as they wish.

The other way we seek to help churches or individuals is to lay on a series of training days on various aspects of the Christian life, especially on subjects related to Christian healing. Some would be on Saturdays, some on Tuesdays or Thursdays, usually not more than two a week. Occasionally a course will extend over two or three days. The subjects include Christian Healing, Christian Counselling, Inner Healing, Healing of the Memories, The Wholeness of Creation, Drug Addiction, Bereavement, Living Alone, Marriage, Family Life, The Church and the Medical Profession, Prayer, Healing of Relationships, Witness at Work. There are also Days of Quiet similar to a Retreat. The Bishop of Tewkesbury, Jeremy Walsh, led a very helpful one for three days early in the life of the Centre. The subject he chose was "The fruit of the Spirit", an important complement to the gifts of the Spirit. The qualities of love, joy, peace, patience, kindness, goodness, faithfulness, gentleness and self-control, that gradually grow in a Christian are, in fact, a description of Christ's own character.

The setting and surroundings of the Manor are very helpful and therapeutic, with an extensive garden, lovingly tended by volunteers; also the surrounding farmland, sometimes with lambs gambolling and skipping in their exuberant new life and always sheep safely grazing in the adjoining fields.

Usually over two hundred people pass through the Centre during a week, sometimes more. One of the great needs that soon became apparent was for on-going Biblical teaching about living the Christian life. As we are in the business of meeting needs, we wondered how to do this. After prayers we eventually devised a course of six teaching days on the second Saturday of the month. We encouraged people to book in for the whole series of six, which, after a break, would be followed by a further six and then another. There was such a response that we had to hold them in the large barn and limit the numbers to 130 people. As with other day courses, they begin at 10 a.m. and finish at 4 p.m., with coffee, ploughman's lunch and tea provided. The opening worship is sometimes led by the "Vision" music group. For these, as for some of our other day courses, we have been able to obtain excellent nationally-known Christian teachers and speakers. As with other courses, we always seek to provide people with an opportunity for prayer and ministry as required towards the end of the day.

At our various courses and other activities we meet some people with time, skills and the Spirit of the Lord. If it seems right, we encourage them to join our band of helpers, but never to the detriment of their own church. A day course that I was helping to lead was attended by a lovely young couple, Tim and Karen. We broke into groups for the afternoon session and Tim happened to be in my group. I was quickly aware that he had skills in prayer and ministering in the power of the Holy Spirit. So afterwards I invited him and Karen to come and take part in our service of Christian Healing the following Wednesday. They have been helping in various ways ever since and have revealed or developed other skills like teaching, preaching and counselling. As they were in a spiritual wilderness at the time, Harnhill has been a great blessing to them and their children.

From the first we have sought to have a good relationship with the medical profession. Some of the local doctors have been very supportive and helpful and have suggested to some patients that they come to see us, and in one or two cases even brought patients to us personally. One young local doctor used to join us for a while at the 7 a.m. prayers on Tuesdays and Thursdays and, when he could, he came to help at our Wednesday evening healing sessions, assisting with the laying-on of hands with prayer. Unfortunately he has now moved to London, but another, more senior doctor and his wife help regularly at our healing services. Doctors and consultants from further afield have also been in contact with us. One doctor from Canada contacted me and came to see the Centre before it was opened, asking many questions and taking literature away with him. Two years later he was over here on holiday again and spoke at one of our Wednesday evening services, telling of how he had helped to start a ministry of healing in his church and some of the wonderful things that had happened. He still keeps in touch.

One eminent heart surgeon from the United States, a Roman Catholic, over here on holiday, came to our service. Having difficulty getting in, he stood at the back straining to see everything that went on. Afterwards, over a cup of coffee, he grilled me for nearly an hour, not sceptically, but wanting to know everything that happened: the sort of questions I asked, the sort of cases that came, the sort of prayers we prayed. He was anxious to learn anything he could that would be of help to his patients. When he returned to the USA he sent a very handsome donation towards paying off our deficit.

One of the outside commitments I continued after my involvement with Harnhill was the chairmanship of the Gloucestership Support Group of the National Initiative in Evangelism. It was an ecumenical committee for encouraging evangelism of every kind in the country. One of the main things we did was to organise a rally each year somewhere in Gloucestershire. One year we took part in the 250th anniversary celebration of the ordination of George Whitfield, which had taken place in Gloucester Cathedral. We hired the Thomas Riches Grammar School in Gloucester which George Whitfield had attended, although the school is now on a new site on the edge of the city. My second name, and the one by which I am known in my family, is Whitfield. My mother's family are supposed to have some connection with George Whitfield's family, although it cannot be by direct descent as George did not have any children. But I was very happy to chair and to introduce the day. Canon Alan Holloway, organiser of the Whitfield celebrations, spoke of the significance of George Whitfield and the Great Awakening of the 18th century. He was followed by an American Methodist, especially over for the celebrations. Whitfield had spent much of his life there and played a great part under God in the Great Revival in the USA.

We had brief accounts of fascinating evangelistic happenings across Gloucestershire. For instance, one young couple told of what they were doing in Gloucester Prison, contacting and visiting young offenders there, leading some of them to the Lord, having them to stay in an old rented house when they came out, so as to continue their ministry to them, and helping the ex-prisoners get established in civilian life. In the afternoon we had workshops on practical aspects of evangelism in various spheres of our society. I led one on "Christian Healing" which led to invitations to a number of churches.

The following October, with virtually no money, we hired a big hall on the other side of Gloucester for Barry Kissell to bring a team from St. Andrews, Chorleywood, to lead a day of renewal. Harnhill was now open and a few were able to come from there. The team from Chorleywood brought a lovely music group and we had some beautiful worship and praise as well as teaching and ministry.

Towards the end of the lunch break a young woman came up with a lovely fair-haired baby. She was one of twins, but was much smaller than her sister and had eczema on her face: "Did I think there was a chance of Barry

Kissell praying for her healing?" - I replied that I was sure there would be, that he was bound to have a time for prayer for various needs towards the end of the afternoon. If she stayed by the door, she could nip out and fetch her child from the crèche when it started. Those who know Barry Kissell will realise that you can never bank on what is going to happen. It depends on what he hears the Holy Spirit saying to him. The afternoon started with some prayer and then Barry started speaking. Before long he suddenly stopped and moved into a time of ministry with prayer and laying on of hands. I nodded to the young mother and she went out to fetch her child. She only took a few moments, but when she got back, Barry had got us all praising and worshipping again. I signalled for her to come and have the spare seat next to me at the very front of the hall: there was standing room only at the back. She came and we continued to sing. Her lovely baby reached out her arms to me and so I took her as I sang, looking lovingly down on her face with its eczema blotches. I suddenly had the thought: "Pray for her healing now!" So I stopped singing and prayed something quite simple, like: "In the name of Jesus I rebuke this eczema. Be healed in the name of Jesus." Then I continued to pray quietly in tongues and watched in amazement with the mother as the eczema blotches just disappeared in a matter of moments and the skin became perfectly normal. I gave the child back to the mother. We continued praising God with very full hearts and wet eyes. When something like that happens, one is conscious of the sovereign working of God's Love and Grace, and that it is nothing to do with one's self. One is just full of adoration of God with a sense of great humility to be privileged to witness such an event. Many more people were blessed before the end of the afternoon.

A few weeks later the mother came up to Harnhill. Her other child had developed painful eczema in the crutch. Two ladies of the team prayed for her and the same thing happened. God is wonderful: the God who, through Jesus, promises fulness of joy and abundant life.

CHAPTER 14

GROWTH AND HARVEST

Ababy soon becomes a child and a child develops into a fast-growing youth. A plant or young tree, once established, quickly grows. This was true of the Harnhill Centre. Exactly a year after the first service of Christian Healing in the church, we had to hold the service in the large barn on June 3rd 1987. At the service the week before, some people had to stand in the church porch and so the move was planned. This was just as well, because the next Wednesday twenty people came by coach from Cardiff and the congregation in the barn was over one hundred. Within a week or two it was a hundred and fifty! God saw to it that our team of helpers was also growing and soon we were having twelve or more couples ministering prayer and the laying on of hands round the edge of the barn.

When we had initially considered the property, we were delighted that the large range of outbuildings were included in the sale. We did not then realise just how essential the large storage barn would become. The team had cleared it and roughly whitewashed the interior. They placed a simple rough altar surmounted by a large wooden cross. Soon, extra lighting and heating were installed and a sound re-inforcement system with a loop for those hard of hearing. We were given an organ in addition to the piano. Later the Youth Camp and then the Art Week were to provide some appropriate wall-banners.

Increasingly the day courses were also held in the barn as the numbers attending grew and the conference room in the house could not accommodate them.

I have already mentioned the conversion of an old wash-house behind the manor into accommodation for Ian and Ann. As well as an outside door, conveniently it also had a connecting door into the office where they spent most of their time. Their accommodation included a spare bedroom which was useful as an extra counselling room or emergency overnight accommodation. Other improvements were going on from time to time: modifications to the bookstall to give more shelf space, extra cupboards in the corridor for coats and storage, stacking chairs, trestles and improved furnishing.

We were clear that the growth of the Centre needed to be matched by the spiritual growth of the team, individually and collectively. The prayer times together continued to be every bit as important as when we were struggling to get the centre going. It was also important to pray for and minister to, each other's needs as well as those outside. This we did. It was also right to take every opportunity to continue the team's training. We benefited a great deal ourselves from some of the courses and speakers we had at the Centre and occasionally would ask a speaker to spend part of his or her stay just sharing with the team. We continued to benefit from the Wholeness Through Christ courses, Lee Abbey, John Wimber Conferences and the like; one or two of the team going at a time. A family evening together of both inner and outer teams was held once a month for fellowship and praise, for sharing and training. In between, a circular letter from the house team to the outer fellowship kept everyone abreast of news and developments. A quarterly Newsletter to Friends and those further afield had begun before we opened.

By 1988 our debts were paid off and we could proceed with further expansion. It had been envisaged from the beginning that we would need more residential accommodation, mainly of single guest rooms and preferably on the ground floor for those who found stairs difficult. Moreover, additional residential accommodation was needed to make the Centre financially viable. Originally we had thought of converting an outbuilding called "Nag's Stable", but in prayer and discussion it became clear that it would be far better to use another area. Plans were therefore drawn up to develop an old shippen, a range of low outbuildings in a large courtyard behind the Manor. This would provide six extra single guest rooms, one for a disabled person with a suitably equipped bathroom attached, a staff bed-sitting room, a counselling room, a new laundry and a small sitting room. Sandy Vearncombe got busy again on a new Appeal, this time for £120,000. Almost immediately we realised that this sum was considerably too low as we decided it would be best to enlarge and improve the kitchen while we were about it. The ultimate cost was nearer £160,000. The work was begun that November and owing to the mild weather and the enthusiasm of the builders, completed ahead of schedule by the end of June 1989. The workmanship was a delight; the new blended beautifully with the old. Everyone was thrilled with it. It now needed furnishing.

That spring, Catherine Pither, having reached retirement age, moved from being a member of the house staff to becoming a valuable member of the outer fellowship. Her place was taken by Diane Salkeld, though with different responsibilities. The housekeeping was taken on by Hilary Kent, who was now free from her part-time teaching which she had continued for a while when she first came to Harnhill.

I first got to know Diane Salkeld in Israel. For years I had been leading parties to the Holy Land, Oberammergau, Steps of St Paul, Seven Churches of Asia, Steps of St Francis. It was one way of getting to these places myself as well as being a wonderful means of developing Christian fellowship. This party was being jointly led by myself and John Perry and his wife Gay from Lee Abbey. We had led others together.

Diane is an attractive brunette in her fifties. I remember talking to her as we walked from one biblical site to another. She told me she had recently been widowed, how her husband Peter had died painfully of cancer, but how pleased she was that he had come to know Jesus as his personal saviour in the last 18 months of his life and how he had received a beautiful vision before he died, reassuring them both of his being welcomed in heaven. She also told me how she was training to be a Reader and we talked of that. I encouraged her to come to some of the courses at Harnhill when she could, which she did from time to time. Hugh asked her if she would come and help in the kitchen at Harnhill for a week while Ruth Warrington was away in Australia for her young sister's wedding. Cooking was not the way Diane wanted to serve the Lord, but she came, although she was rebellious inside.

This was dealt with when Bishop Ban It Chiu came to speak. At the end of the Wednesday healing service he went and ministered to Diane in the kitchen. She soon found herself resting in the Spirit on the floor. Others of the team drifted into the kitchen and soon they too were resting in the Spirit on the floor; fourteen altogether, singly and in pairs including the Bishop!

The following weekend (three days later), at a Readers' retreat on the theme of Sacrifice, God began speaking to Diane about the possibility of going to work at Harnhill as part of the residential staff. At the same time God was speaking to a number of the team in the same terms; in fact, I had visualised that possibility when I had met her in the Holy Land. In one way the idea thrilled Diane, in another she felt unworthy. She also realised the sacrifice involved in giving up her home and living in a one room bed-sitter. When she thought of Christ's sacrifice for her, she gladly accepted Hugh's invitation on September 7th 1988. She did not move in permanently for some time, eventually taking over Catherine's room the following spring. Her responsibilities, as well as in the kitchen with Ruth, are in the office, taking over there when Ian and Ann are on days off or away - she also helps Hugh with his letters and programme planning. This latter aspect of her work has continued to grow. Like the rest of the house team, Diane helps with leading the worship or preaching at the services and with counselling as required. Being a Reader, she also helps with the services in the local group of churches as required by the Rector. She always looks so right at Harnhill: her radiant smile cheers everyone up. She was well integrated into the inner team by the time the new wing was finished.

Although the new wing was completed by the end of June 1989, the courtyard it enclosed was still a pile of rubble. The Trustees had decided that the extension was costing so much that the landscaping of the courtyard and provision of a spacious patio should be left until the following year. However, during July, as we were planning the opening ceremony of the wing, some of the team, notably Theresa Vearncombe, and Ann Campbell felt strongly that the patio at any rate should be done to provide somewhere for people to stand at the opening. As for the money, one of the team offered an interest free loan to cover the work. The Trustees were quickly consulted, estimates sought and the cheapest one accepted. The contractor promised to finish the job during August. He was as good as his word.

Meanwhile, day by day, and week by week, the life of the Centre went on as people came with their various needs. A woman came to one Wednesday evening healing service, who had just been diagnosed as having inoperable cancer. Tim and Karen prayed with her that the cancer would melt away. A day or two later she had to see the consultant again with a view to deciding what treatment, if any, they could give her. Fresh x-rays were taken. After a while the consultant, looking puzzled, came to her and said:

"I don't understand what has happened. It is as though the cancer had just melted away." He had used the very same words as in Tim and Karen's prayer.

It would be misleading to imply that everyone who comes to Harnhill receives such dramatic and instant healing. Thank God some do. Others receive gradual healing; others find Jesus as Saviour for the first time or the empowering of the Holy Spirit. Few, if any, go away without some blessing from God. His desire is to bring us all to wholeness of body, soul and spirit in His time and in His way, through the saving love of His Son and the power of the Holy Spirit.

On Sunday 3rd September 1989, just three years after the Centre was opened, we celebrated the Official Opening and Blessing of the New Wing. All the money had been raised, though there was about £56,000 outstanding in interest free loans. The response had been quicker this time and charitable trusts were more ready to give, with the Centre now established and functioning. Within another two or three months the loans too had been repaid.

Catherine Pither headed up organising the arrangements for the opening, which went very smoothly in a real atmosphere of joy and celebration. Over two hundred invited guests arrived for the 2.30 p.m. start, and all but a few managed to pack into the barn. After some lively introductory worship led by the house team and "Vision", Bishop Chiu, who was with us again leading a weekend of refreshment, gave a fascinating address. He urged us not to set limits on what the Holy Spirit could do through the Centre or through any of us. He illustrated it with a little alarm clock which played a great variety of different tunes in order to wake one up. In like manner, the Holy Spirit could work in a great variety of ways and we should expect Him to do so and not just in the ways he had worked before. The Rural Dean and local Rector, Canon Peter Jeffries, led us in prayers of thanksgiving and dedication. In the closing hymn the Bishops and house team went out to the New Wing for Bishop Chiu to cleanse and dedicate each room with Holy Water and prayer. At the end of the hymn the rest of us went across on to the new patio and stood facing the New Wing for the Bishop of Gloucester to dedicate and bless it, and formally declare it open. Letty and I then cut the third birthday cake as a preliminary for tea. It was good to have Ruth Warrington's parents there from Australia, whom we had known all those years ago.

What of the future? It is not envisaged that there should be any further increase in the number of resident guest rooms. At present we can accommodate fourteen guests. Those staying very often comment on the peace of the place and the love they receive. They also express gratitude for the family atmosphere. This might be difficult to maintain if we had more staying and, in any case, the reception rooms would become overcrowded. Fragile and hurt people are often intimidated by large numbers.

The improvement that is most urgently needed now is for better accommodation for the Warden/Chaplain, his wife and family. This must be undertaken as soon as the right place can be found in the grounds and planning permission obtained; one suggestion has already proved unsuitable. This would also release more accommodation for the other staff. The number and composition of staff is something that is likely to change from time to time.

The other major development envisaged after that is to utilise fully the barn complex of buildings and make it a self-contained conference unit. They are listed buildings and so the outside appearance must be preserved. Nevertheless, the addition of two small galleries in the barn would bring the seating capacity up to two hundred. The other buildings lend themselves to the provision of a spacious reception area and bookstall with adjacent toilets. Also there is space for the provision of buffet lunches and more counselling rooms. This would save the Manor house from the additional wear and tear it receives when we have large training or teaching days. Moreover, the need for such teaching in the Christian Faith and how to live and minister in the power of the Holy Spirit is likely to increase as more and more churches come into renewal during this decade of evangelism.

In St John chapter 15, Jesus makes it clear that growth is for fruit bearing which comes from abiding in Christ, pruning, loving one another and receiving the Holy Spirit.

In the Old Testament, several passages speak of the righteous being like a tree planted by water that remains green even in desert conditions and bears fruit constantly, eg. Jeremiah 17.8 Ezekiel 47.1-12,

"This water flows from the sanctuary, the presence of God and in addition to the fruit from the trees, the leaves are for healing." Jesus offers such living water to the Samaritan woman at the well (John 4), and to everyone when, at the Feast of the Tabernacles, he invites anyone who is thirsty to come to him (John 7.37). St John adds in verse 39 that Jesus was speaking of the Holy Spirit who had not yet been given because he had not been glorified, a clear reference to Pentecost. Peter and John, like Jesus himself, did not begin their ministry until they had been filled with the Holy Spirit. Then it began immediately with power, Peter preaching with such effect that 3,000 were converted and baptised, Acts 2. In the next chapter Peter commands, in the name of Jesus Christ of Nazareth, the man crippled from birth, to walk; to the astonishment of all he accompanies the apostles into the Temple, leaping and praising God.

Growth in buildings and facilities, in numbers of staff and in those coming to the Centre, is for one thing: fruit bearing. That will happen through those who abide in Christ, accept pruning, love one another and are constantly replenished with the Holy Spirit.

When looking out across a desert, everything seems completely barren. When rain comes, it is obvious that there has been life there all along as unexpectedly green shoots appear. The spiritual bareness of much of our national and international life is there for all to see. However, dormant seeds are there waiting to be brought to life, growth and fruit bearing by those who abide in Christ, love one another and allow the full flow of the living waters of God's Holy Spirit to fill them and overflow to others.

By God's grace, an abundant harvest can spring from the desert.

POSTSCRIPT

The Harnhill Centre was all but completed when we went for our usual family holiday in the Western Highlands of Scotland. One day, high up in the hills on my own with a trout rod, I stopped for my simple lunch of a sandwich, a chocolate bar and an apple. As I gazed at the superb view across the sea loch towards the Torridon mountains, I thanked God for the beauty and majesty of His creation and then for, at last, bringing the Centre into being after all the hard work in faith. Then, rather rashly, I asked: "What next, Lord?" - The answer came simply and quickly: "Write a book."

The execution of His bidding was not so simple. It was impossible in the busy daily routine of the Centre to tackle such a task. So, after about eighteen months, we took a cheap one-month winter package-holiday in Tunisia and I sat on the balcony and started to write. Later, I was asked to speak at a church in Majorca, where we stayed with Pamela Clarke. She offered us her home in Puerto Pallensa for a fortnight the following year while she was in England. We accepted and I was able to complete and revise the manuscript.

Next, I had to get it typed, before checking passages with people whom I had written about. I was praying about it in a small group of people during one of our courses and someone I hardly knew said: "I'll be glad to type it." So Elizabeth Boyd painstakingly turned manuscript into corrected typescript. Later, Jerry and Jo Baldwin captured it on a computer, with a few more corrections.

Finding a publisher during the recession proved difficult until Christian Brann took it on with great enthusiasm, making some excellent improvements in the process. John Elliott, author and scriptwriter, who once lived in Chedworth, kindly edited the book. Finally, Bishop John Perry fulfilled an earlier promise and wrote the Foreword. I am very grateful to all these friends and to the many others whose names appear in the book, for enabling me to answer the Lord's bidding. Most of all I am thankful for His help.

Now the book is finished, I am bound to ask: "what next?" For my part I should be content just to work on the extensive improvements and development programme which is just beginning at the Harnhill Centre.

BIBLIOGRAPHY

What next for *you*, the reader of this book? I hope that it has given you food for thought on your Christian progress through life. Reading about the experience of others who have gone before us can give us strength and encouragement. I have set down, in this further reading list, some titles I have found helpful and can commend to you.

The Christian Life.

Title	Author	Publisher
You are my God		
Fear no Evil }	David Watson	Hodder & Stoughton
Discipleship		
A Way through the Wilderness	Jamie Buckingham	Kingsway
My Father is the Gardener	Colin Urquart	Hodder & Stoughton
Anything You Ask	"	"
Chasing the Dragon	Jackie Pullinger	"
Come, Holy Spirit	David Pitches	"
The Church in the Market Place	George Carey	Kingsway
Listening to God	Joyce Hugge	Hodder & Stoughton

Christian Healing.

Unexpected Healing	Jennifer Rees Larcombe	Hodder & Stoughton
Your Healing is within you	Jim Glennon	"
Healing	Francis Mac Nutt	"
The Prayer that Heals	"	"
The Love that Heals	Andy & Audrey Arbuthnot	Marshall & Pickering